"Autarchy" in Clement of Alexandria

Christian Heritage Rediscovered

The Series, as the name suggests, is meant to focus on Christian Faith & Living vis-à-vis topics like Literature & Poetry, Indigenous Philosophizing, Ethical response towards Agriculture, Health & Healing, Science & Technology, Eco-feminist Theology, Sociological approach towards Human Rights, Law & Politics, Arts, History of Ideas, Ancient Civilizations, Cultural Contiguity, Religious Cosmologies & Mysticism, Footsteps of famous Theologians, World Peace & Harmony, Global Capitalism, Network Marketing, Cybertheology, Population & Demographics, Epigraphic Studies, Contextualized Education, and many others. We welcome a Mss. on any topic/s mentioned, whether they are original works, scholarly monographs, collections of conference papers, revised dissertations, or translations of historical documents. Through the Series we, the Publishers, are striving to put forward published works that may help Institutions, Academic Bodies, Researchers, Scholars and the World at large in furthering their respective knowledge and understanding on the concerned subject. We welcome your comments on our efforts and further suggestions on how we can foster the upcoming thought provoking theologically grounded books.

Christian Heritage Rediscovered - 65

"Autarchy" in Clement of Alexandria

Socio-Economic and Ecological crisis Re-examined in Indian Context

Anish John

CWI

Christian World Imprints™

First Published in 2018 by

Christian World Imprints™
Christian Publishing & Books from India
H-12 Bali Nagar, **New Delhi-110015**
info@christianworldimprints.com
www.ChristianWorldImprints.com
Phone: +91 11 25465925

ISBN: 978-93-5148-275-8 (HB) ISBN: 978-93-5148-276-5 (PB)

Cataloging in Publication Data--DK
Courtesy: D.K. Agencies (P) Ltd. <docinfo@dkagencies.com>

John, Anish, 1984- author.
"Autarchy" in Clement of Alexandria : socio-economic and ecological crisis re-examined in Indian context / Anish John.
pages cm. -- (Christian heritage rediscovered ; 65)
Includes bibliographical references.
ISBN 9789351482758 (HB)
ISBN 9789351482765 (PB)

1. Clement, of Alexandria, Saint, approximately 150-approximately 215. 2. Autarchy--Religious aspects--Christianity. 3. Economics--India--Philosophy. I. Title. II. Series: Christian heritage rediscovered ; 65.

LCC BR115.E3J64 2018 | DDC 261.85 23

Printed in India.

To the Glory of God

&

Memory of Appa..

Contents

Acknowledgement

Glory and honour be to the source of all knowledge, the one Triune God.

This research work forms a significant part of my efforts towards Masters in Theology and is actualized in book form by the extensive support of several enlightened individuals. Let me extend my gratitude towards Met. Dr. Mathews Mar Severios, who guided this research, with his unparalleled knowledge into the subject and comprehensive thought. I also respectfully bear in mind the guidance and support received from Met. Dr. Youhanon Mar Demetrios, Rev. Dr. K. G. Pothen, Rev. Fr. Dr. K. M. George, and Rev. Fr. Dr. V. S. Varughese (Registrar, FFRRC).

These efforts were materialized through extensive engagements and encouragements of my teachers at Federated Faculty for Research in Religion and Culture, St. Thomas Orthodox Theological Seminary, Nagpur and Orthodox Theological Seminary, Kottayam during the course of academic grooming. My heartfelt gratefulness also to the Librarians and staff members at UTC, Bangalore; TMAM, Manganam; MTTS and OTS, Kottayam for facilitating my naive readings. My learning in fellowship of friends and batch mates especially, Fr. Jomon John, Rev. Justin, Selvam Christuraj, has been immense. Also, very importantly, this work wouldn't have been materialized without the constant support and empathy of my family and the divine joy I get from of my little angels, Sarah & Rachel.

Big thanks to my publisher Christian World Imprints, for agreeing to publish this work as a text under Christian Heritage Rediscovered series.

In Christ,

Anish John

List of Abbreviations

2Cor	Second Corinthians
A.D.	Anne Domini
B.C.	Before Christ
Brih.	Brihadaranyaka Upanishads
Deut	Deuteronomy
Isa	Isaiah
Matt	Mathew
Paed.	Pedagogues
Phil	Philippians
Strom.	Stromateis
Trans.	Translator/Translators

Abstract

This book is an attempt to discover the philosophical concept of *Autarchy* (Self Sufficiency) in the thought of Clement of Alexandria as a paradigm for constructing a *Greed line* in Indian Context. WCC has been working on the *Greed line* (an upper limit, curbing greed) and drawing paradigms from the Bible, economics, social and structural analysis. However, an attempt to delve into the Patristic resources is also generally lacking. This work on 'Autarchy' also tries to address the issues of poverty, income disparity and social sensitivity in an Indian context. It unearths the Indian Philosophical and Gandhian thoughts too in specific towards this goal. The existing global culture is often plagued by the passion to consume and possess. The unreasoned boast abounds that the good life is found in accumulation idea that "more is better".

Autarchy in Clement of Alexandria catalyzes an inner detachment or self-sufficiency mode in life. This self-sufficiency is not self acclaimed, rather it is a gracious gift in union with the providence of God. Autarchy calls forth a refined attitude to wealth, material goods, to self itself. *Autarchy* traverses from Platonic, Aristotelian, or Stoic ideal to a virtues reward in communion with and in God. The Trajectory encompasses a shift in paradigm. *Autarchy* is not the product of human efforts but Grace, received in communion with God.

Moreover, the intend of this research work on *Autarchy* is definitely not an attempt to standardize or regulate the upper limit of an individual's needs. Needs vary but the blind exploiting & consumerist attitudes are alarming to human as well as the nature.

Autarchy evolves into an ethical and moral principle for individuals, corporate to tackle issues of greed, consumption, ecological crisis and poverty, especially in Indian context.

Introduction

The economic and financial breakdowns, bankrupt nations and alarming ecological degradation have all constantly raised concerns for linking Poverty, Wealth, Ecology and its legitimacy. Rising Governmental policies and checks against unethical financial gains, unaccounted income by individuals or corporate all directs towards a more subtle, ethical and social change. Greed and legitimate use of wealth seemingly a spiritual and moral imperative, now seeks discussion even for structural changes in national or transnational policies. As Dr. Rogate Mshana puts it, "The intertwined financial, economic and ecological crises are rooted in greed." (In the Foreword, *The Greed Line*, Final Report published by WCC).

The religious fabric of Christianity owes an unprecedented responsible attitude to the concerns of Greed, poverty and wealth. This concern is a responsibility of *diakonia*[1] not of any exclusivist superior claims in a Pluralistic context. World Council of Churches has extended discussions focusing on poverty, wealth and ecology since its 8th Assembly at Harare, 1998 directly with AGAPE (Alternative Globalization Addressing People and Earth) process. Also, the WCC's motto of preferential option for people in poverty remains relevant today.[2]

However, the Early Christian wealth of Social sensitivity and Philosophical tradition of Patristics remain unexplored in

1 *Ministry*; active service, done with a willing (voluntary) attitude.

2 Athena Peralta & Rogate R. Mshana, eds., *Linking Poverty Wealth and Ecology* (Geneva: WCC Publications, 2013), vii.

contemporary discussions. Christian Church possesses in its literature an abundant and incomparable treasure. But, it is an inheritance that must be reclaimed by each generation.[3] The concept of 'Autarchy' (*Autarkia*) in Clement of Alexandria catalyzes thought towards a new ethical and moral paradigm to counter greed. In the Indian context of widespread poverty, economic disparity and unrestrained exploitation, *Autarchy* as in Clement would enable a culture of *enough* and help constructing a *Greed line.*

Title

"Autarchy" in Clement of Alexandria: Socio-Economic and Ecological crisis Re-examined in Indian Context

Basis of the Research

This study is an exploration into the concept of *Autarchy* in Clement of Alexandria towards establishing a *Greed Line* for Indian Context.

Basic framework

The concerns of wealth and poverty, its legitimate purpose, catalyzed by recent economic recessions have all raised alarms for constructing a "just" and "enough" economic model. The issues of structural greed and poverty are being persistently discussed in economic consultations at national and international levels. The World Council of Churches had opted, "Economy of Life: Overcoming greed to eradicate poverty" as a major theme for ecumenical conversations at its 10th General assembly held at Busan, 2013.

The word greed itself is generic and pejorative. However, in economic parameters it is an interesting fact that there exists a bench mark for the minimum level of consumption or per capita income of a person referred to as 'poverty line'; on the contrary, the upper limit of consumption remains unbounded. *Greed line* is thus the upper limit of a legitimate consumption or share of goods. Wealth is

3 John Ernest Leonard Oulton and Henry Chadwick, trans. and eds., *Alexandrian Christianity*, Vol. 2 of *The Library of Christian Classics*, edited by John Baille, John T. McNeill and Henry P. Van Dusen (Philadelphia: Westminster Press, 1954), 9.

essentially seen as a blessing in Christian understanding. However, it also seeks a greater responsibility and commitment towards the cause of the poor.

While the biblical tradition does not provide direct guidance for the contemporary effort to identify a "wealth line" or a "greed line", it points to a relatively consistent normative framework for considering the social responsibility of wealth and condemning the greedy accumulation of property and wealth as idolatry. This framework was adapted and developed further in the early church.[4]

Autarchy or self-sufficiency is an approach widely discussed in cynic and stoic philosophy; however, primarily explored in Christian perspective by Clement of Alexandria. His works are especially noted for their intellectual proximity to stoicism, illustrated by his use of the concepts such as *Autarchy* and neutrality of goods. Alexandria was one of the largest cities in the Roman Empire, a cosmopolitan place with considerable wealth, especially through trade, and highly developed culture of learning. Given this context and his own background, Clement addressed himself to the educated and reasonably well off members of the community. While he attacked the conspicuous wealth and luxury of the elites, he did not question wealth as such, nor did he believe that poverty in itself was meritorious. His approach to the question of poverty and wealth is inner detachment from wealth, whose main purpose is to provide for the basic needs of daily life, and the focus on *koinonia*, the praxis of sharing property and wealth for the benefit of the whole community. Since wealth is a gift from God, it should be used to meet the needs of those who lack the means for their sustenance.

Martin Hengel summarizes his teachings in the following terms: Clement counters the extravagance of the well-to-do... with reasonable, disciplined moderation which is guided by the "Logos"...and gives full share to the neighbor in need. The aim of this instruction by the Logos is not a flight from the world, but a reasonable, moderate and at the same time generous use of worldly goods, thus in clement traditions of Jewish wisdom, Stoic ethics and the message of the New Testament, combine in the specific situation

4 Kondrad Raiser, "*Theological and ethical considerations regarding wealth,*" *WCC Ecumenical Review* (October, 2011), 280.

of the Alexandrian church in a new synthesis which is to point the way forward for the later church.[5]

Clement of Alexandria in his *Paedagogus* (2, I, 132) defined: "Just as the measure for the shoe is the foot, so is property related to the needs of the body". God created the world in order for us to use it; however, we earn material goods so as to achieve autarchy. *Autarchy* breeds good men for society, especially when it is accompanies by love. (see also *Stromata*, iv, 5), *Rich Man's Salvation (XIV).*

Clement does not seem to outrageously condemn wealth and luxury such as, for example, fine clothes worn by Christians and their attendance at public baths, rather he rejected the excessive use of it (a kind of inner detachment). Thus while interpreting the parable of Lazarus and the rich man, Clement warned the wealthy of the danger for their salvation. According to our Lord's teaching, he urged the rich to give generously to the poor, contending that this injunction shows Christian charity. To such well-off Christians he addressed his later volume *Can the Rich be Saved*? Clement advised his readers not to let life's material goods or greed get in the way of better concerns. He argued that property itself does not bring a man closer to God.

The researcher intends to consider certain parameters or indicators for evolving a better understanding of *autarchy* which are:

- The Economic behavior
- Money and Interest
- Wealth: accumulation, distribution and Retention
- Social structure of economy
- Koinonia
- Gluttonous consumption, etc.,

Significance of the Research

The growing global economic and financial crisis, far spread income disparities have all raised alarms to develop some theologizing as part of our struggle to overcome greed and injustice. The Indian background–its economical, political and social disparities all relate

5 Kondrad Raiser, "*Theological and ethical considerations regarding wealth,*"*WCC Ecumenical Review* (October, 2011), 282.

perfectly to the conditions dealt with by Clement of Alexandria. In Indian context special emphasis on 'plain living' which helps in cutting down wants and promotes self-sufficiency is the basic guiding principle of Gandhi's economic thought. An exploration in Indian context remains a valid position for *Autarchy*.

Also, absorbing insights from the Church Father in his efforts during the 3rd century Alexandrian Christianity would surely guide us towards a profound progress for establishment of a *Greed line* (largely as a moral concept) in Indian context.

Purpose of the Research

The intent of this research is to explore the wealth of Patristic "autarchy" in Clement of Alexandria towards establishing a paradigm for "greed line" in Indian socio-economic context.

Methodology adopted

The research is mainly analytical and reflective. It will be analyzing the works of Clement of Alexandria to trace the concept of "Autarchy" and its means, towards establishing a *Greed line* in Indian context.

Hypothesis

Exploring *Autarchy* as an ethical and moral concept towards a new paradigm for constructing *Greed line* in Indian context.

Division into Chapters

Chapter 1: Clement of Alexandria: Life and Thought
Chapter 2: Autarkia in context
Chapter 3: Greed line and Paradigm of "Autarchy" for Indian Context
Chapter 4: Conclusion

Scope and Limitation

- The concept of *Greed line* is developed and understood largely at an ethical and moral level, devoid of any attempts to define it as a pure economic term or pattern (as *poverty line*) *Greed line* is thus the upper limit of a legitimate consumption or share of goods in an ethical and moral terms.

- This study is an attempt to build a pattern for establishing a *greed line* in Indian context of far spread economic disparities especially in "Gandhian" thought of self sufficiency.
- The study lacks availability or use of original texts by Clement of Alexandria, and is limited to the available translations (mostly in English).

This book also includes as appendix, few research papers by author in the area of Patristic Theology and of contextual relevance for students of Theology. Anthropological Theology, Gandhian Thought, Ecclesiology, Reason & faith, are some of the essential categories dealt herewith.

Previous Research

No direct research material is available to the extent of researcher's knowledge. However, linking discussions are traced in the article by Kondrad Raiser, "*Theological and ethical considerations regarding wealth,*" in *WCC Ecumenical Review* (October, 2011) and in the Final report and supporting studies published by WCC in 2014 (as a report of the Greed line study group, WCC), titled "The Greed line" edited by Rogate R. Mashana and Athena Peralta.

Chapter 1

Clement of Alexandria
Life, Influences and Thought

1.1 Introduction

Clement of Alexandria is a towering figure of the Early Christian age (2nd A.D). He was an architect of Christian Hermeneutics and Biblical Scholarship par-excellence. Jerome's high praise that "of all Fathers he (Clement) was the most learned" (*Epist., LXX, 4*), speaks for itself. He very well treaded the path of synthesizing Greek Philosophy and the Christian message. Clement believed that "Philosophy is of divine origin"[6] and that was unimaginable to the contemporary Christian mind of his times. An outstanding exponent of the theology of the Alexandrian School, believed to be the first Christian university.

The wide range of writings of clement posses a wealth of Greek philosophical concepts wed into Christian faith. And the concept of "Autarchy" evolves in such a philosophical context for Clement as a virtue of Christian faith, an ethical morale.

6 John Ernest Leonard Oulton and Henry Chadwick, trans. and eds., *Alexandrian Christianity*, Vol. 2 of *The Library of Christian Classics*, edited by John Baille, John T. McNeill and Henry P. Van Dusen (Philadelphia: Westminster Press, 1954), 19.

1.2 Alexandria

It is generally believed that, Christianity must have taken root early at Alexandria.[7] As W.H.C Frend describes, "Alexandria had already begun to be a centre for the Christian mission by 180 A.D. The city was the main port for a varied trade between the eastern Mediterranean, the Red sea, and beyond the Gulf of Aden across the Indian Ocean to the Malabar Coast. There were also contacts with an important town just south of Pondicherry (*Poduca*) where quantities of fine Roman tableware (*samian* pottery) and amphorae have been found."[8] It was the second city of the Roman Empire, the centre of flourishing trade and commerce, with a population about half a million. This included a large Jewish populace. The learned Jew Philo, elder contemporary of Paul, mentions that the Jews in Alexandria and all Egypt totaled about a million. And it was the home of that Hellenistic Judaism of which Philo's works are an outstanding monument.[9]

As Norman Russell, gives a realistic view of the situation, explaining that the Church in Egypt (Alexandria) has left no archaeological evidence dating from before the fourth century to help us trace its race and development. Written sources are also few Eusebius offers no information for the period before the last decade of the second century beyond a bare list of bishops with an indication of their date. It is only with Bishop Demetrius (189-232), in whose episcopate Pantaenus, Clement, and Origen were active, that Eusebius has reliable material to draw on. This near-invisibility of the early Egyptian Church may be explained by the vicissitudes of the once large Jewish community that in the earliest years must have formed the Church's matrix.[10]

Alexandria was also a cultural centre of the highest importance and was one of the leading intellectual centers of the Roman world.

7 Oulton and Chadwick, trans. and eds., *Alexandrian Christianity...*, 15.

8 W.H.C. Frend, *The Rise of Christianity* (Philadelphia: Fortress Press, 1984), 286.

9 Henry Chadwick, *Early Christian Thought and Classical Tradition* (London: Clarendon Press, 1966), 15.

10 Norman Russell, *The Doctrine of Deification in the Greek Patristic Tradition* (New York: Oxford University Press, 2004), 116.

It had two important libraries, and students gathered there to study literature and especially science–among its alumni we hear of Euclid (450-380 BCE) and Galen (C.E 200). In fact it was what we should nowadays call a university town. The library is believed have been open for public since the time of Augustus. There was also the Serapeum, with its significant 'daughter library', and many schools, both public and private, which attracted students from all over the Mediterranean.[11] Alexandria was also a religious centre. Worshippers of every creed were to be found there. The pagan deities, the Roman Emperors, the local native cults, all had their shrines there.[12]

1.3 Clement of Alexandria: *Theologian Par Excellence*

In Clement' of Alexandria (c.150-215), the outstanding "interpreter of Christian faith in the early centuries, we encounter a true bridge-builder between Christian faith and secular culture.[13] Clement was a traveler, always moving on. He invites Greeks to desert to God's side and to enjoy the danger of change (*prot* 10.93.2). In his quest for knowledge, he left home and travelled to teachers around the eastern Mediterranean, moving from Italy to Egypt.[14] Clements's life work was a war, waged on two fronts; to approximate Christianity to notions drawn from Graeco-Oriental syncretism and heterodox Judaism.

1.3.1 Birth and Early Years

Very few facts are directly known to us concerning the life of Clement of Alexandria. His title comes from the city which was the scene of all his important work; but an early tradition spoke of him as being an Athenian by birth, and this may be correct. The date of his birth can be fixed roughly at 150 A.D. We are told nothing of his parentage or early training. It seems clear, however, that he was not a Christian

---

11 Norman Russell, *The Doctrine of Deification in the Greek Patristic Tradition* (New York: Oxford University Press, 2004), 117.

12 Majorie Strachey, *The Fathers without Theology* (New York: George Braziller Inc., 1958), 136.

13 http://www.fatherkmgeorge.info/Books/gospel.htm (29/10/15).

14 Eric Osborn, *Clement of Alexandria* (U.K: Cambridge University Press, 2005), 1.

to begin with. He is so well acquainted with the mystery cults that there is a strong probability that he had been initiated into some of them. We have it on his own authority that he wandered through many lands and heard many teachers. Six of these he singles out for mention, though not by name; they were "blessed and memorable men," who spoke "plain and living words." Doubtless all of them were Christians. The last of the six, who was "first in power," and whom he found in Egypt, is almost certainly Pantaenus, then head of the Catechetical School at Alexandria.[15] A mention of the School of Basilides, usually considered a Gnostic teacher is imperative at this juncture. Like that of Clement the intellectual background of Basilides was a mix of Stoic ethics and Pythagorean theology, later widely regarded as characteristic of the Platonist Philosophy of the Hellenistic age.[16] Clement staunchly objected the deterministic scheme of salvation and the implied ethical consequences in Basilides. However, as Norman Russell points out, Clement did study Basilides and his son Isidore's writings carefully.[17]

In the famed passage Clement tells us about his education (*Strom., I, II*): "This book is not written to show off my skill as a writer; it is rather that Iam treasuring up notes for my old age, a remedy for forgetfulness. They are intended simply as a picture and rough sketch of those clear and living teachings and of those blessed and truly honorable men whom I was privileged to hear. Of them one was an Ionian who taught in Greece. Others were in Magna Graecia [I.e., Southern Italy]; of them one came from Coele-Syria, the other from Egypt. Others lived in the East; of these one was an Assyrian, one a Palestinian Hebrew. After I met the last (who was first of them in importance) I abandoned further search, having discovered him hiding in Egypt. A truly Sicilian bee, he drew honey from the flowers in the meadow of the apostles and prophets, and implanted in the souls of his pupils pure knowledge."[18]

15 G.W. Butterworth, *Clement of Alexandria* (London: Harvard University Press, 1919), xi-xii.

16 Russell, *The Doctrine of Deification in the Greek Patristic Tradition* ..., 119.

17 Russell, *The Doctrine of Deification in the Greek Patristic Tradition*..., 119.

18 John Ernest Leonard Oulton and Henry Chadwick, trans. and eds., *Alexandrian Christianity*, Vol. 2 of *The Library of Christian Classics*, edited by John Baille,

For Clement it was at Alexandria that his wanderings for quest of knowledge ceased at least spatially. Soon he became a presbyter of the Church, and taught in Alexandria for more than twenty years, succeeding Pantaenus[19] as head of the Alexandrian School. Later, at the outbreak of persecution under Severus[20] in 202 C.E, he left Alexandria, never to return. We get one more glimpse of him; in 211 C.E., he was the bearer of a letter from Alexander, afterwards bishop of Jerusalem, to the Church at Antioch. In this letter he is described as "Clement the blessed presbyter, a virtuous and esteemed man... who upheld and extended the Church of the Lord." Alexander was one of Clement's old pupils, and a fellow-pupil with the great Origen. Clement must have died not long after this letter was written; for the same Alexander, writing to Origen a few years later (around 215), speaks of him together with Pantaenus as "those blessed men who have trodden the road before us."[21] Clement with his first hand experience and interactions with the contemporary world around remains for ever a *wider Christian Philosopher –Theologian.*

1.3.2 Philosophy and Influences

Clement has been seen variously by different interpreters, and this owes to the versatile thought pattern. One is instantly reminded of St. Paul's words, "To the Jews I became as a Jew...To those outside the law I became as one outside the law." (I Cor. 9:20-21). Meanwhile, one extolled Clement as a Christian liberal, while another explored his rich store of citations. Many have struggled with his literary form. One was drawn to the richness of his call to piety and perfection. Another discerned a logical pattern, which permeated his thought. More recently, some writers have pointed the depth of his penetration of Plato and others his understanding of true philosophy. However,

---

John T. McNeill and Henry P. Van Dusen (Philadelphia: Westminster Press, 1954), 16.

19 Head of Catechetical School of Alexandria from around AD 180.

20 Septimius Severus, Roman emperor from 193 to 211.

21 Oulton and Chadwick, trans. and eds., *Alexandrian Christianity*, Vol. 2..., xii.

it is truly evident to say that clement, more than any other early Christian writer knew and enjoyed Greek philosophy and literature.[22]

As for Clements's his favorite theme was that the world was prepared by Greek philosophy for the Christian religion. Among all the schools, Platonic, Stoic, Cynic, Pythagorean and even from that of Epicurus, he had something to gain, and except the last mentioned, he abandoned none of them when he found his permanent resting place within the Church. No man of his age knew better what philosophy could provide and where philosophy fell short. And, in so far as he had learned this in his student days, Athens rendered him a great and abiding service.[23]

In spiritual matters Clement called for philosophical exploration and movement: he exhorted Greeks to turn to Christ, to follow Christian morals in every detail of behavior and finally to become wise in the mysteries of Christ. Practical problems drew attention and analysis from his inquiring mind. Despite his criticism of Gnostic theosophy, he followed the flight of Theodotus,[24] exploring new questions and problems. The Christian should never abandon his simple faith, but he should always be moving on in his journey towards wisdom and the likeness of God. Saturated with study of this culture, he belonged to Alexandria, a city which was ruled by it. Clement displayed that heritage as clearly as Tertullian displayed the Roman heritage of Carthage. Alexandria was a cosmopolitan city that had a population of Greeks, Jews, Egyptians, other native Africans and Romans. It had a dominating position in trade. It also had a long literary tradition and a special Platonic tradition which Eudorus[25] represented. Its libraries were central in its learning. Clement quotes more than 300 different literary sources for more than a thousand references to other writers. Jewish-Hellenistic works were also available to Clement. Philo was a major influence, and

22 G.W. Butterworth, *Clement of Alexandria* (London: Harvard University Press, 1919), 2.

23 Rodney A. Whitacre, *A Patristic Greek Reader* (Massachusetts: Hendrickson Publishers, 2007), 7.

24 Theodotus, a follower of Valentinus (an Alexandrian Gnostic).

25 Eudorus of Alexandria was an ancient Greek philosopher, and a representative of Middle Platonism.

minor influences came from Demetrius, Aristobulus, the Sibylline oracles and others. Interestingly, the story of the Alexandrian origin of the Septuagint emerges in a second-century tradition which is found in Clement and Tertullian, Justin, Irenaeus and elsewhere. Clement exhorted pagans to turn to Christ with kerygmatic fervor. His language was tied closely to the text of scripture which was ever in need of transposition from vision to metaphysic. Logic for Clement always helped to expound scripture and to defend its truth.

1.3.3 Biblical Hermeneutics

The writings of Clement are considerable in extent, and remarkable in character. Hardly a page can be found without some Old and New Testament reference or exposition.[26] His achievement began from a grasp of divine love as the core of the Christian gospel. God is not God unless he is both father and son, for the divine being is the love which joins father and son. God is love and the revealed mystery of this love is the gospel. Clement's faith in one God is expressed in both philosophical and biblical terms. God is one because he is one and nothing but one (a simple unity), and because he is one and universal.[27]

From this scheme he explained the duality which he found in the Johannine account of God, who is father and son, God and word etc. Clement used the relation between simple and complex unity, between father and son, claiming that in philosophy as in the bible they could not be held apart. The reciprocity, which joined them, is central to his thought. He speaks (*Paed 1.5.24.3*) of the great God who is the perfect child, of the son in father who is father in son. He quotes Is. 9:5, 6 where the Holy Spirit tells him of the great God who is perfect child in newness and perfection. Elsewhere, he speaks of the undefiled God, who has taken the form of man, who is the servant of the father's will, who is both word and God, who is in the father and at the right hand of the father and who has the form of God as he has the form of man (*paed* 1.2.4.1). One can see how Clement

26 G.W. Butterworth, *Clement of Alexandria* (London: Harvard University Press, 1919), xiii.

27 Eric Osborn, *Clement of Alexandria* (U.K: Cambridge University Press, 2005), 2.

follows the Platonic logic of simple and complex unity (*Parmenides* 137c–142). God is the first and oldest first principle and the cause of all things. Nothing can be predicated of him, for he is neither a whole nor a collection of parts. He has no limit, form or names, so all the names we give him are improper. We choose the best names to support our understanding and to indicate the power of God. He cannot be proved because there is nothing prior to him and he is known only by the grace and the word which proceed from him (*Paed.* 5.12.81f). Yet the same God, as divine logos, is the creator and sustainer of all things.[28] Interestingly, Clement doesn't array into writing a commentary on scripture but exploring the logos theology of the Fourth Gospel, the drama of salvation drawn from Paul and a sense of the relation between God and man as it runs through the whole of scripture. Scripture sets for him the problems of theology and controls the formation of his thought. He is a Platonist as well as a biblical theologian.[29]

Eric Osborn explicates the features of Clement's Biblical expertise when he writes, 'For one of his best modern interpreters, Clement's fusion of prophecy and Plato opens the way to a biblical theology.' Again, Clement finds in scripture the progress of the soul to God. To sum up, in 'his profound and concrete religious sense, in the richness of his theological ideas, in his reflection upon the nature of symbolism which is present in the natural world and especially in scripture, by his continual investigation into the problems of the knowledge of God and in the relation of Greek philosophy and Christian faith', Bluntly put he goes beyond exegesis to biblical theology.[30]

1.4 The Trilogy and other Writings

It is believed that Clement replaced Pantaenus as the head of the so called 'catechetical school' in Alexandria and began teaching sometime in 190, but was forced to relinquish the role and flee

28 Robert Rainy, *The Ancient Catholic Church* (New York: Charles Scribner's Sons, 1902), 89.

29 Eric Osborn, *Clement of Alexandria* (U.K: Cambridge University Press, 2005), 75.

30 Osborn, *Clement of Alexandria* ..., 75.

Alexandria during the persecutions of Severus in 202. It was probably during this time that he wrote the works that are collected under his name.[31]

As Eric Osborn explicates, "Movement marks the plan of Clement's writing" (a detailed salvific movement also discussed under next heading). Clement follows the logos who exhorts pagans to desert their falsehood for the truth of God, instructs them in the ethics of Christian practice, then goes on to teach the true knowledge of the mysteries of Christ.[32] Following this plan, Clement's major works form a trilogy: (a) The Exhortation to the Greeks *(Protrepticus)*, (b) The instructor *(Pedagogues)*, (c) The Miscellanies *(Stromateis)*. The Title *Stromateis* was not uncommonly used in Clement's age for writings without any strict order and containing varied subject-matter. In the manuscripts there are eight books of the *Stromateis*, and Eusebius of Caesarea thought the whole work was complete in the eight books before him. But the eighth book was evidently not intended for publication, and consists of notes of a preparatory nature on which Clement draws in the first seven books. Probably it was appended to the incomplete work after Clement's death. As to how many books Clement meant to write we cannot comprehend. Towards the end of Book VII (cf. also VII, 89) he writes of continuing further. Also, the surviving minor works compound the sense of movement. There is a sermon on the salvation of the rich man (*Quis dives salvetur*? and a fragment on patience to the newly baptized. The former written to reassure his wealthy and cultured Christian pupils that Christ condemned only the wrong attitude to wealth, not wealth as such.

Numerous fragments of other works are quoted in later writers, and the manuscripts also preserve two works which throw important light on Gnosticism entitled "selections from the Prophetic Sayings"(*Eclogae Propheticae*) and "Epitomes from the Writings of Theodotus and So-called Eastern Teaching of the Time of Valentinus"(*Excerpta ex Theodoto*). Of the latter there is an edition with English translation and notes by Dr. R.P. Casey (1934). It is

31 Andrew C. Itter, *Esoteric Teaching in the Stromateis of Clement of Alexandria* (Boston: Brill Publications, 2009), 7.

32 Osborn, *Clement of Alexandria* ..., 5.

scarcely intelligible without an extensive commentary.[33] Eusebius cites works which are lost, except for fragments: *On the Passover, On Fasting, Against Judaisers, On Providence.*[34]

1.4.1 Kerygma: The Divine Movement and Economy of Salvation

Eric Osborn in a very subtle and apt manner describes the Divine movement, "From invitation (*Protrepticus*) through instruction (*Pedagogues*) to perfected humanity (*Stromateis* VII) is as decisive as are the earlier ages of the plan of salvation."[35] Clement in his writings ever uses the language of movement to describe God, salvation and humanity. Clement's Exhortation to the Greeks is a lyrical work beginning with a description of the gospel as the new cosmic song which supplants the old songs of the Greeks and which can turn stones into men. The new song overcomes the dullness of those whose hearts are petrified against truth. The exhortation culminates in an offer of salvation.[36]

Further, the beginning of Clement's thought, as for other second-century theologians, is the primitive Christian Kerygma, which speaks of a good and only God, and of his plan of salvation, which comes to perfection in Christ and may be received by all. Yet it seems at times that the Kerygma was overlooked while emphasis was philosophical deliberations. However, for Clement Kerygma is pivotal and it emerges at the beginning of *Protrepticus* (4.59.2); Homer is ordered to be silent in the presence of those who have received the divine likeness of a God who dwells with them and feels for them. These are the chosen generation, the royal priesthood, and the peculiar people of God. They have learned everything from him who came from above and they have come to know the economy, the plan of salvation, of God the supreme disposer (*Prot.* 4.59.3).

33 John Ernest Leonard Oulton and Henry Chadwick, trans. and eds., *Alexandrian Christianity*, Vol. 2 of *The Library of Christian Classics*, edited by John Baille, John T. McNeill and Henry P. Van Dusen (Philadelphia: Westminster Press, 1954), 17.

34 Oulton and Chadwick, trans. and eds., *Alexandrian Christianity*..., 5.

35 Osborn, *Clement of Alexandria* ..., 55.

36 Osborn, *Clement of Alexandria* ..., 31.

With this knowledge, they are able to walk in newness of life. The economy joins the old with the new and begins with God's creation of the universe out of nothing by his pure volition, an act which he alone was able to achieve (*Prot.* 4.63.3). The Kerygma begins from God and continues in his economy.[37] The unity of the divine plan declares God's unchanging purpose, which is to save the flock of men. It was for this reason that he sent the good shepherd and acted in ways consistent with the fulfillment of his plan (P*rot.* 11.116.1). In accommodation to his Greek readers, Clement turns first to the account of the philosophers. Their opinions about God are largely wrong (prot 5); but some philosophers have spoken the truth.[38]

1.5 Critical Evaluation

Works of Clement since late 18th century has been critically assessed and questions raised on its authorship. Clement's 'trilogy' of major works raises questions which drew close attention of the academia during the first half of the twentieth century. The crucial passage in the first chapter of the *Pedagogues* distinguishes between the divine logos who invites men to salvation (*protreptikos*), then guides them to right action and the healing of their passions (*paidagogos*) and finally teaches, explains and reveals first principles, clarifying symbolic and ultimate statements (didaskalikos). None have questioned the first two elements of Clement's threefold economy. Also, the *Protrepticus* and *Paedagogus* bear the names which denote their functions. Traditionally, the *Stromateis* were taken to be the Didascalus. De Faye in 1898 claimed that the *Stromateis* were too unsystematic to be the final work of Clement, who had intended to write a systematic treatment of Christian knowledge but was forced by his complex environment to write a preliminary work which justified the use of Greek philosophy. The stimulus for the *Stromateis* lay in the caution of many Christians towards Greek philosophy which heretics had used (it was thought) to the detriment of the faith. De Faye was

37 Osborn, *Clement of Alexandria* ..., 32.

38 Osborn, *Clement of Alexandria* ..., 32.

dominated by a belief in 'systems' which was characteristic of his day.[39]

The views of De Faye were very soon attacked by Heussi,[40] who gave forward an amendment of the traditional view. Again, in 1925, Prat[41] proposed a diverse version to re-establish in part the traditional claim for the *Stromateis.* Munck went into greater detail and provided grounds for believing in two trilogies: *Protreptikos, Paidagogos, Didaskalos*; and *Stromateis I–III, Stromateis IV–VII,* and *the Physiologia.* Munck[42] claimed that Clement did not produce the final work of either trilogy. However, this attractive solution appeared too systematic for Lazzati, who divided the works into two broad categories, Firstly, those intended for private instruction, and again those directed to the general public. The seven books of the Stromateis and the three commentary works were esoteric. The *Protrepticus, Paedagogus* and *Quis dives salvetur*? were meant for the general public. Yet another interpretation was proposed by Quatember, who argued impressively that Clement's trilogy referred to three stages of instruction, not to three written works (triology).[43]

Osborn points out another notable literary comment on Clement from S. R. C. Lilla, who devotes a footnote to the puzzle of the *Stromateis.* Lilla inclines to the view of de Faye and disagrees with Me´hat: 'The Stromateis, though dealing in many sections with gnosis, never examines in detail such arguments as cosmology or theology, which represent the content of the higher gnosis and which would fit in very well with the logos didaskalikos, but rather touch them en passant.' Such a view, however, plays into the hands of E.L Fortin, for whom Clement's brevity is exactly the means by which the 'higher gnosis' is communicated. Lilla concludes that Clement's reference to a subsequent work, dealing with cosmology and theology, points to the proposed Didascalus.[44]

---

39 Osborn, *Clement of Alexandria* ..., 5-6.

40 C. Heussi's work, 'Die Stromateis des Clemens Alexandrinus und ihr Verha¨ltnis zum Protreptikos und Paidagogos'.

41 F. Prat's work, 'Projets litte´raires de Cle´ment d'Alexandrie.

42 J. Munck, Untersuchungen u¨ber Klemens von Alexandria.

43 Osborn, *Clement of Alexandria* ..., 5-6.

44 Osborn, *Clement of Alexandria* ..., 9-10.

Another critical view of the *Stromateis* was put forward by J. Ferguson, who claimed that they are what the title suggests, a scrapbook of notes in which Clement stored his material.[45] Clement bit off more than he could chew, and the *Stromateis* constitute a collection of ideas which never cohere as instruction for Christians seeking higher knowledge. Ferguson claims that on occasions Clement mentions his intentions for the Didascalus: for instance, he will give some account of first causes, some account of the Greek mysteries and will write more on the true Gnostic. However, according to Ferguson these things are postponed and never written. In the *Stromateis,* Clement is only concerned with scraps; he is merely 'composing a piece of exhibition oratory...a kind of sketch of words and people, lacking sharpness and vitality.'[46]

Among some recent discussions Kovacs has discussed the 'divine pedagogy' of Clement, drawing attention to his ability to teach simultaneously at different levels. Clement needed to reach the different spiritual levels of students and yet communicate the higher gnosis for those capable of apprehending it. The *Stromateis* are compared with scripture: 'As the logos has carefully designed the literal and symbolic levels of Scripture so that the same text can simultaneously teach students on quite different levels, so Clement chooses the versatile genre of the miscellany.' *The Stromateis* are designed to sort out 'advanced students' and to take them through a program of instruction.[47]

1.5.1 Photios' *Bibliotheca*: Critique

Another prominent attack on Clements writings was in the 9th century by Photios I. Photios, who was the Patriarch of Constantinople from 858 to 867 and from 877 to 886; found eight highly controversial, 'heretical', opinions in Clement's *Hypotyposeis* that he outlined very briefly, without any extensive quotations from the original document (which itself makes the arguments weak) in his book *Bibliotheca*. The eight 'erroneous doctrines' found by Photios and examined by

45 Osborn, *Clement of Alexandria* ..., 9-10.

46 Osborn, *Clement of Alexandria* ..., 9-10.

47 Osborn, *Clement of Alexandria*..., 11.

Ashwin-Seijkowski in his book *Clement on trial* are the metaphysical doctrines that eternal matter and ideas exist (Chapter I) and that there were many worlds prior to Adam's creation (Chapter II) ; the theological teaching concerning two Logoi of the Father (Chapter III); the creaturely nature of the Son of God (Chapter IV), and a docetic[48] understanding of Christ (Chapter V); and the anthropological ideas of the transmigration of souls (Chapter VI); a shameful construal of the creation of Adam and Eve (Chapter VII), and the notion that angels sexually impregnated Women (Chapter VIII).[49]

Piotr Ashwin-Siejkowski in his book examines each 'error' listed in the 109th codex of Photios' '*Bibliotheca*' in depth, using evidence from Clement's existing work to consider the likely accuracy of Photios' critique. Focusing on these eight 'heresies' offers a unique opportunity to illuminate what in terms of post-Nicene orthodoxy are Clement's most problematic opinions, setting them in the context of their original philosophical and theological frame.[50]

1.6 Conclusion

Clement of Alexandria stands out in early Christian history and Patristics as a Theologian par excellence. Unparalleled authenticity and novelty in deliberations, forerunner in contextual theologizing, moral theologian, and towering figure in Christian ethics are just few adjectives to the great persona. From very minute aspect of Christian living to profound theological thoughts are found in colossal works of Clement. Clement is described precisely as "a Platonist, a Philonist, and a Euhemerist, a close student of the Bible, of Gnostic masters, and of ecclesiastical writers, and a well-informed commentator on mystery cults and Egyptian religion, but his teaching is more than simply a blending of these influences."[51]

---

48 Doscetism is the idea that Jesus Christ only appeared to be human, and not in real.

49 http://ext.sagepub.com/content/124/8/405.extract# (15/11/2015).

50 https://www.academia.edu/835571/Monograph_Clement_of_Alexandria_on_trial_the_evidence_of_heresy_from_Photius_Bibliotheca (10/11/2015).

51 Norman Russell, *The Doctrine of Deification in the Greek Patristic Tradition* (New York: Oxford University Press, 2004), p. 123.

Clement was introduced to many Greek philosophical schools such as Platonic, Stoic, Cynic, Pythagorean, and Epicurean thought at an early phase in life. And When Clement became a Christian he denounced Epicureanism, though he never abandoned the whole of Greek philosophy. He bridged the gap between Christianity and Philosophy, to make "Philosophy a handmaid of Theology."[52] He eventually became the leader of the Alexandrian church and one of the Alexandria's most influential theologians. He also left a theological legacy that is still influential and sought after.

As rightly summed up in the words of Robert Rainy, Clement brought to the service of Christianity a full and ready mind. No one of his time has quoted so largely from the store of Greek literature. He loved beauty and goodness, and he found their traces everywhere; accordingly, he counted on a response from human hearts, when appealed to in the name of beauty, and goodness, and God. The position in which he was placed, and the work he had to do, called upon him to present Christianity to his hearers as the crown of all worthy human thoughts: it was a creed in harmony with all that men had found to be valid, supplying what men had felt to be lacking. Clement believed all this; he devoted his resources to make it good; and in so doing he set the type of the earlier Alexandrian Christian teaching.[53] The remarkable synthesis of Philosophy into the Christian thought premise in Clement of Alexandria leaves a trail to be pursued with passion to trace 'common grounds' in contemporary context.

---

52 William Wilson, trans. and eds., *The Writings of Clement of Alexandria*, Vol. I of *Ante Nicene Christian Library*, edited by Alexander Roberts and James Donaldson (Edinburgh: T & T Clark), 366.

53 Robert Rainy, *The Ancient Catholic Church* (New York: Charles Scribner's Sons, 1902), 162.

Chapter 2

Autarkia: In Context

2.1 Introduction

It is remarkably important to build the trajectory of Autarchy (*Autarkia*) in its contemporary context. It springs in the Philosophical context and moves further into the sphere of Early Christian writings.

Alan Kreider enlightens us of early Christian conception of *Autarkia*, "Contentment (Autarkia) was the believers' antidote to covetousness. It was not a position of poverty or need; it was a position of enough. Contentment was God's two-handed provision, both for the individual and for the neighbor. "if we have food and clothing," Paul wrote, "with these we shall be content" (I Tim. 6:8). But not just enough of these basics for oneself; there must also be enough to give. The reason to work, according to Paul, is to "be able to give to those in need" (Eph. 4:28). Contentment was a road to freedom: "Keep your life free from love of money, and be content with what you have" (Heb. 13:5).[54]

Kreider further explains the difference between the Greek and Christian idea Autarkia, he explains, "when Pagan Greeks used the word "Autarkia" (contentment) they meant individual possessing resources enough to stand alone. But the post resurrection disciples

54 Alan Kreider, *Social Holiness* (Eugene: Wipf and Stock Publishers, 2008), 189.

of Jesus knew that they could only experience contentment in sufficiency if they also were committed to a second principle – *koinonia*. This Greek word, often translated "sharing", or "fellowship", means "making common."[55] Since time immemorial, sufficiency and equality, contentment and sharing –have been the basis of economic life of the early Christians.

2.2 Philosophy: Handmaid of Christianity[56]

As B.A.G Fuller observes, 'Beginning as an incident in the general pooling of metaphysical and religious interests characteristic of the epoch, Christian philosophy grew and flourished, while the main stem withered, till it became the tree of which all metaphysical speculations were the branches for the next thousand years.' This new growth, however, differed in one fundamental aspect from the old. Contemporarily understood, the service of the ancient gods was one of perfect philosophic freedom and autonomy. As long as their existence was not denied-and even that could be safely challenged save in religiously hidebound communities like that of Athens – freedom of criticism and speculation was undeterred by interference from priests or populace. Heresy was a thing as yet unknown. Indeed, the service of the traditional religion was not only liberty but, license in speculation, since the over fertile soil of polytheism sometimes encouraged philosophy to a rank and fantastic growth unrestrained even by the bounds of common-sense and sober thought. Still, such license was preferable to the straits in which philosophical speculation now found itself. Christianity was founded on revelation – another concept unknown to the Greeks, except perhaps in the clairvoyant murmurings of the oracles, which, however, vouchsafed no solutions to metaphysical problems. But now the true version of the nature and the constitution of Reality, which in the past had been sought by the use and tested by the standards of reason, was made manifest once and for all to all mankind by God speaking at sundry times and in diverse manners by the Hebrew prophets and in these latter days

55 Kreider, *Social Holiness…*, 189.

56 Title from, *The Miscellanies* Chapter V.

by Christ.[57] This phase reduced philosophy into an inferior state of existence.

Moving on, the early Christian writings such as letters of Paul and documents like the Epistle to the Hebrews and the Fourth Gospel show, however, followers of Christ now included men of considerable talent prone to metaphysical speculation. It furthermore depicts that these men were interpreting His status as the incarnate Son of God in the light of contemporary Neo-Pythagorean and Neo-platonic Philosophy, and more especially by the help of the concept of the Logos, the medicating and creative word or wisdom of God upon which Philo had laid such stress; e.g. "In the beginning was the Word, and the Word was with God, and the Word was with God, and the Word was God." (St. John 1:1). But even so, the relation of the Son to the Father and of the Holy Ghost to the Father and the Son was still a wide-open question, and many other important theological problems were still more vaguely formulated and further from definite solution.

The next two centuries of Christian thought were abound with various conflicting speculations and deliberations, amongst which it became impossible to make a distinction between the tares of future heresy from the wheat of future orthodoxy. As Fuller concludes "Indeed, what was finally accepted as revealed truth was the product of a relentless struggle for existence among the most diverse opinions, eventuating in a survival of the fittest determined in part by philosophic considerations and on philosophic grounds. The same was to hold true for future centuries. It was only as some speculations rather than others received in the councils of the Church a majority vote inspired by the Holy Ghost, that they were regarded and became Christian verities."[58]

It is remarkable to notice the peculiar and exotic flavor of the myriad Gnostic speculations, which drew both upon Neo-Platonism and the Oriental religions for their fantastic doctrines. The Gnostics tried to treat Christianity much as Proclus tried to treat polytheism. The Valentinian Gnostics, for example, regarded it as a kind of

57 B.A.G. Fuller, *A History of Philosophy* (New York: Henry Holt and Company, 1938), 328-329.

58 Fuller, *A History of Philosophy* ..., 330.

terminal product of an incredibly complicated system of emanations and intermediary beings descending from the ineffable One to a sensible world whose imperfections and very existence are due to forces of evil rather than of good. This extreme dualism of God and the universe they paralleled with an equally extreme opposition of the human soul to the world and the flesh and the devil. The soul is fallen so low that her redemption would be impossible had not Jesus, the mightiest of the divine emanations or aeons, taken pity on her and descended into the sensible world to show her the way back to God. This return is affected by the observance of a system of rites and sacrifices, endowed with magic efficacy.[59] And gradually in these circumstances, some discrepancies as magic and astrology emerged as large as they did in contemporary non-Christian religious and philosophical context.

Dualistic ideas of the Universe interpreted in moral or cosmological terms of light and darkness were held in uneasy tension with the fundamental conviction that God was One. These speculations were also affecting individual conduct.[60] The dualistic and the diabolistic interpretation of the Gnostics persisted as a powerful movement, which in the form of Manichaeism we find still very much alive at the end of the fourth and the beginning of the fifth centuries.

As Fuller puts it, gradually in the meantime, controversy that was helping formulate Christian truth was centering on the question of the Trinity and particularly in the relation of the Son to the Father. For instance, at the other end of the scale from those who contended that Christ was simply a great prophet were the Patripassians who identified him with the Father and maintained that in his crucifixion the Father himself suffered death upon the cross. There were also the Sabellians who regarded Father, Son and Holy Ghost as merely three aspects of one and the same divine person. Again, there was the party later represented by Arius, who considered the Son a created being of different but similar substance. Still again, we have the Montanists who protested against the development both of worldliness and

59 Fuller, *A History of Philosophy* ..., 331.

60 W.H.C Frend, *The Rise of Christianity* (Philadelphia: Fortress Press, 1984), 204.

theology within the church and believed themselves to be the special beneficiaries of a new descent of the Holy Ghost, under whose leadership they were restore primitive Christianity. Finally there were those who under the guidance of a saner Neo-Platonism than inspired the Gnostics were marching slowly but surely towards the formulation of the Nicene Creed.[61]

In keeping these last in step two men, Clement and Origen played an indispensable part. Both were members of the church at Alexandria, learned in contemporary philosophy and sympathetic with other religions, which, unlike their less broad-minded brethren, they regarded not as essentially false and diabolic but as such imperfect intimations of the nature of Reality as religious experience and reason unenlightened by revelation could achieve. Both were strongly influenced by Philo's doctrine of the Logos in their discussion of the relations of the Father and the Son, and were hardened advocates of his allegorical method of interpreting, which Origen, at least, carried so far as almost to deny verbal inspirations and to reduce the outer and historic aspects of the Incarnation and redemption to signs and symbols of an inner all-embracing cosmic process. They had to commend Christianity to men sharing the culture of the time, and interested in the questions which it raised. And these men laid the foundations of Christian theology and exhibited Christianity to be as tenable against the philosophies which claimed to embody all that was discoverable of the good, the true, the fair.[62]

Of the two thinkers Clement was perhaps the more dominated by Neo-Platonic thought. Thus, he strikingly anticipates Plotinus in his doctrine of the transcendent and ineffable nature of the Father, and his teaching that the Son is the divine mind of the Father, through which the Father creates and in which he becomes conscious of what he creates. Also in Clement can one notice profound influence of Philo's Platonism. For him also God was absolutely transcendent, "Unity but beyond unity, transcending the monad."[63] Neo-platonic is Clement's insistence that the fate of the soul is not determined in

61 Fuller, *A History of Philosophy ...*, 332.

62 Robert Rainy, *The Ancient Catholic Church* (New York: Charles Scribners's Sons, 1902), 163.

63 Frend, *The Rise of Christianity...*, 371.

this life, but at the end of a process of probation and purification, terminated, in his opinion, only by the Last Judgement.[64]

At the same time Clement did not believe in "original sin." Mankind is not infected by Adam's fall. Each human soul comes into the world as perfect as Adam and suffers only for own abuse of free-will. Finally Clement shows his Hellenic heritage by his opposition to excessive moral dualism. Indeed, the distinction that he does make between the higher and the lower life is founded on the Aristotelian opposition of the supermoral, contemplative activities to the "lower" activities of practical reason with which ethics deals.[65] Even though a man's sin be scarlet and he die unrepentant, he cannot here and now exclude himself from the possibility of future redemption. Sin, Clement attributed, very much as Proclus did, to the misuse of man's power of choice between good and evil. (cf. The Miscellanies Book II, Chap. XV, "Sin then is on my part voluntary,...*Sin shall not have dominion over you; for ye are not under the law ,but under grace*"). But whereas Proclus and the Gnostics regarded the power to choose evil as a mark of imperfection, Clement felt it to be, in man at least, a sign of perfection. In this way he dealt with the Gnostics' argument that Adam was created imperfect and therefore must be, along with the rest of the universe, the work, not of God, but of an evil creator. Clement had an optimistic view of human beings and their relation to God. The world was created by God and therefore was good. Man and Woman had been made in the image of God, and had the means within themselves to progress toward God. (Cf. *The Miscellanies*, Book V, Chap. XIV, *Exhortation to the Heathens*, Chapter XII). There was no "natural evil" and no impassible categories of spiritual Men. Christ was the Teacher (*Paidagogus*) of humankind rather than Illuminator of the few. "Nothing in excess," the Stoic maxim was also Clement's bon mot. Riches were neutral gifts, depending on how they were used. To Clement wealth was a matter of stewardship.[66]

---

64 Fuller, *A History of Philosophy* ..., 332.

65 Fuller, *A History of Philosophy* ..., 333.

66 Frend, *The Rise of Christianity*..., 371.

2.3 Autarkia: In Greek Philosophical Context

Autarkia as a Greek philosophical concept was widely regarded as a mark of the human good, happiness (*eudaimonia*). The word *Autarchy* comes from Greek *autarkia*, derived from *autos* meaning 'self' and *arkeo* which in its passive form means 'be satisfied, content' or rather can be paraphrased as "out of my own power". A life is self-sufficient when it is worthy of choice and still lacks nothing in itself. However, what makes a life self-sufficient – and thereby happy – was a matter of controversy since ages. For instance, the Stoics believed that the mere possession of virtue would suffice; The majority of the Fathers spoke for a state of autarky, or the modest self-sufficiency of man, characterized by the consumption only of necessary goods. The celebrated Stoic Epictetus (XXXIII, 7) wrote: *Take only what is absolutely necessary for your body, that is food, drink, clothes, a house and slaves. Anything else, which is for show or for pleasure, you should relinquish.* The remarkably consistent, but little known, writings of the Fathers on this subject also deserve examination at some length. For example, Clement of Alexandria in his *Paedagogus* (2, I, 132) denned this state by saying:

Just as the measure for the shoe is the foot, so is property related to the needs of the body. God created the world in order for us to use it, however, we earn material goods so as to achieve autarky. Autarky breeds good men for society, especially when it is accompanied by love.

Again, Aristotle and the *Peripatetics*[67] insisted that virtue must be exercised and even, perhaps, accompanied by material goods. There was also a debate among later Greek thinkers over whether a self-sufficient life is solitary or whether only life in a community can be self-sufficient.[68] The ideal man or perfect being project finds mention in earliest Greek philosophical discourses and Self sufficiency (*autarkia*) is a virtue for ideal or wise man as noted in Stoic philosophy. They believed man must free himself of all passions; one must cultivate renunciation and endurance to strive after self-

67 *Peripatetic is* an adjective ascribed to followers of the Greek Philosopher Aristotle.

68 Robert Audi, ed., *The Cambridge Dictionary of Philosophy* (Cambridge: Cambridge University Press, 1999), 221.

sufficiency.[69] *αὐτάρκης* is admirably illustrated by Plato in Republic (*Repub., 369 B*) as, *οὐκ αὐτάρκης, ἀλλὰ πολλῶν ἐνδεής*."The origin of the city, then," said I, "in my opinion, is to be found in the fact that we do not severally suffice for our own needs, but each of us lacks many things. Do you think any other principle establishes the state?" "No other," said he.[70]

Epicurus agrees with Aristotle's suggestion that happiness must be, as far as possible, stable and in our control, independent of external circumstances. Such a conception of happiness appears in the Platos' Gorgias.[71] Socrates suggests, that the person who lacks (or needs) nothing is happy; he satisfies his desires because he has adapted them to the available resources. Callicles disagrees, claiming that happiness requires not simply complete satisfaction of desires, but the maximum level of satisfaction, requiring expanded desires. Again Epicurus notes that, we count self-sufficiency as a great good, not so that we will have only a few things at our disposal, whatever happens, but so that, if we do not possess many, we well find the few sufficient, since we are genuinely persuaded that the people who have the pleasantest enjoyment of luxury are those who need it least, and that everything natural is easy to obtain, whereas what is difficult to obtain is empty. And so plain food brings us pleasure equal to a luxurious diet, once all the pain resulting from need is removed; bread and water produce the highest pleasure when one who needs them takes them...and so, when we say pleasure is the end, we do not mean the pleasures of profligates and those that consist in gratification, as is supposed by some who are ignorant, or disagree with us, or take us up wrongly or dishonestly. We mean being without pain in the body and without disturbance in the mind.[72]

Philo of Alexandria[73] explains self sufficiency and writes (*Teles, frg. 2.12)*, "so if I show you two old men, two poor men, two exiles,

69 Rudolf Bultmann, *Primitive Christianity* (Cleveland: The World Publishing Company, 1963), 138.

70 http://www.pub22.net/avilla/Republic.html (28/12/2015).

71 *Gorgias* is a Socratic dialogue written by Plato around 380 BC.

72 Terence Irwin, ed., *Classical Philosophy* (New York: Oxford University Press, 1999), 331-332.

73 Philo of Alexandria (20 B.C-50 A.D), a Hellenized Jew.

one of whom is quite content and tranquil while the other is in total turmoil, isn't it obvious that it is not old age, not poverty, not lack of citizenship that should be blamed but something else?" Cf. Plutarch, *Cohib. ira 461c*: "we must accustom the body to contentedness by plain living and self-sufficiency, for those who need but little are not disappointed with much." Assimilation to God entails imitating the Divine, while here the goal is a god-like self-sufficiency (Cf. Clement *Paed. 3.1.1)*.

Again, In Leg. 716c-d, Plato had associated assimilation to the divine with becoming moderate and temperate, though for closer parallels we must turn to texts demonstrating Pythagorean influence, e.g., Sent. Pythag. 30: "the one who truly lives like God is the one who is self-sufficient (*ho autarkees*) and without property and a philosopher and regards not to need anything even necessities, as the greatest wealth." Cf. *Ps.- Ecphantus, Regn. 82.7-30* . God who is completely sufficient in himself; God lacks nothing and needs nothing (Det. 54; Spec. 2.38), being "in himself all-sufficient for himself" (Cher. 46; cf. Decal. 81).[74]

A fundamental observation was that "in many respects, achieving self-sufficiency constituted the general philosophy of the Greek world."[75] E.g., Xenophon, Mem. 1.6.10: "to have no wants is divine; to have as few as possible comes next to the divine; as that which approaches nearest to its nature is to the supreme". For Philo, the preeminent embodiment of such an ideal was Moses, who perhaps more than anyone else eschewed material wealth as blind.[76] As Debashis Guha opines, 'The essential nature of the Divine is to be immutable and self sufficient. So, the concept of "*apatheia*" (passionless) is closely related to the Greek idea of "*Autarkia*" (contentment).[77]

---

74 Walter T. Wilson, *Philo of Alexandria* (Netherlands: Brill Publishers, 2011), 105-106.

75 Wilson, *Philo of Alexandria*..., 106.

76 Wilson, *Philo of Alexandria* ..., 106.

77 Debashis Guha, *An Inquiry into the Cases of Pain and Suffering* (New Delhi: Concept Publishing, 2007), 121.

2.4 The Christian Context: A Project of Perfection

Autarkia, or self-sufficiency, is a pivotal theme in the Early Church Fathers, and one of the principles upon which many Monastic orders were also founded. Interestingly, autarchy as discussed above finds its dynamic references in the early Hellenistic philosophies of Cynicism, Epicureanism, and Stoicism. The Stoic virtue of Ideal human essentially requires practice of Autarchy. Its Christian origins however, can be traced strongly to St. Paul's letter to Philipians and other references[78] (C.f Philipians 4:11, *Nestle GNT 1904*, οέχ ὅτι καθ' ὑστέρησιν λέγω· έγώ γάρ ἒμαθον έν οἶς είμι αὐτάρκης εἶναι and 2 Corinthians 9:8; 1 Timothy 6:6).

As George Gotsis and Sarah Drakopoulou Dodd explicate in their work (*Economic Ideas in the Pauline Epistles of the New Testament)*, that for Paul, *autarkeia* must be experienced as an additional consequence of the Divine Grace which is bestowed. However, Paul's description of his own autarkia, in fullness and hunger, in abundance and want, carries Stoic overtones of detachment from the vagaries of his circumstances and fortunes (Phil 4:11-12). On the other hand, **this self-sufficiency clearly is not due to his own efforts, but to God who gives him strength** (4:13). This is exactly where Paul draws an analogy with the community: God's grace is inexhaustible and abundant, thus enabling the believers not only to meet their own material and spiritual needs, but also to excel in every good work, or charity (2 Cor. 9:8). Self-sufficiency, or autarkia, cannot therefore be dissociated from the precept of benevolence or compassion (9:9), evolving into a responsibility of using material goods to the advantage of the needy. Refined and put forth in the 20th Liberation Theology catch word echoing, "Preferential option for poor". In this profound perspective, it does not lead to a mode of living independently of others' needs. Mostly, in Biblical context as in contemporary thought this precept is a necessary means to overcome scarcity, the inadequacy of resources, underlying the numerous food crises and shortages of goods that affected many Roman territories during 44-49 AD, Jerusalem included. Paul's seemingly paradoxical theology of self-sufficiency perhaps needs to be understood in terms

78 E.g. Philippians 4:11.

of the many dimensions and levels at which it operates. Importantly, in the spiritual realm, believers abandon anxiety about wealth and resources, entrusting themselves to God's grace. This results in a (Stoic-like) detachment from the things of this world. Because the material world is narrowed in importance, ritual sinfulness is not so important, and believers are left open to continue their previous employment. This again bestows an additional benefit, through grace of God, of material self-sufficiency and contentment. In the Church, furthermore, voluntary and generous sharing of resources would let the needy, also to meet their material needs. Importantly, self-sufficiency at the level of the religious community has more in common with Jewish traditions of the duty of care for the poor.[79] Thus, Self-sufficiency is wider in its conception of temporal and spiritual/ethical, individual and communal, and it means to some extent, different things in each context, although a coherent general scheme can be perceived. This ideal of self-sufficiency concludes in 2 Thess 3:11-12, where Paul commands those who neglect their duties to attend quietly to their own work and to earn their own living.[80]

2.5 Trajectory of *Autarchy* in Clement

Autarkia or self sufficiency was a special concern of Clement, defined profoundly in Stoic terms, and used to cover categories not only consumption of goods, sexual matters, but also with money, luxury, possessions, sights, speech and evil thoughts etc. (C.f *Strom.* III,59; II,223,5). The extent of vision envisaged by Clement is universal in every context. He was dubbed in the Hellenic tradition, however fully conversant with the Christian tradition. In his trilogy the *Protrepticus, Paedagogus,* and *Stromata,* Clement reveals his own structured approach to a stabilized moral order. At the same time he lays the foundations for a Christian moral doctrine that starts with the need of uprooting sinfulness and replacing it with Holiness achieved through the virtuous path that proceeds in extension from *apatheia* to *autarkia,* firmly Stoic in conception, but working

79 *http://www.hetsa.org.au/pdf/35-A-3.pdf* (28/12/2015).

80 *http://www.hetsa.org.au/pdf/35-A-3.pdf* (28/12/2015).

its trajectory towards the Christian development in the-*Theosis*.[81] He constructs this procedure through an allegorical interpretation of Abraham's ascent of the mountain, based greatly on Philo of Alexandria. Autarkia in Clement is often accompanied with several other profound concepts as Harry O. Maier in his article, *Clement of Alexandria and the Care of the Self* (*Journal of the American Academy of Religion LXII/3*, Vol. 62, No. 3, Autumn, 1994), explains, "*autarkeia,*[82] self-sufficiency, is gained with the help of self-training (*gumnazesthai*[83]) and self-service (*autourgia*[84])."[85]

2.5.1 *Autarchy* and *Theosis*

Gripping is the fact that Clement of Alexandria was the first to use the technical vocabulary of deification, but he did not think it necessary to explain it. Also, no formal definition of deification occurs until the sixth century, when Dionysius the Aeropagite declares: 'Deification (*theosis*) is the attaining of likeness to God an-d union with him so far as is possible.'[86]

Autarchy in Clement of Alexandria blossoms in perfect essence when it is understood in the pivotal concept of ultimate goal, road to achievement of the Divine perfectness-Theosis. Clement (*like Ireneus of Lyons)* saw the human being as possessing the potential for further development and achievement of the ultimate goal: Theopoiesis/*ohmoiosis*. Clements' treatment of *theosis* is much more

81 A Greek word meaning "divinization" or "deification". Theosis is a central theme of Orthodox theology and spirituality, summed up in the familiar statement of Athanasius: "God became human that we might become divine". The closest counterparts to the idea of Theosis in the theologies of the Western church are "mystical union" with Christ and "sanctification".

82 E.g., *Paed.* 1.98.4 (1.149.9-10); 2.128.2 (1.233.3-5); *Strom.* 7.44.5 (3.33.16-17).

83 E.g., *Strom.* 2.60.5 (2.145.18); 7.83.2 (3.59.16-17); 7.44.7 (3.33.26-27).

84 *Paed.* 3.52.1 (1.266.15); in his treatise on marriage, which is no longer extant, Clement states that he has dealt with the ideal of *autourgia* in greater detail (*Paed.* 3.41.3-1.260.19). *Paed.* 1.11.4 (1.149.12-14) describes the Christian as self-sufficient and his or her own servant (*autodiakonon*).

85 http://www.jstor.org/stable/1465211 (10/10/2015).

86 Norman Russell, *The Doctrine of Deification in the Greek Patristic Tradition* (New York: Oxford University Press, 2004), 1.

convincing and high-minded. Like Plato he believes in the idea that man's ultimate purpose is to unite himself with God. This is achieved only when man's will becomes one with God's will. In these circumstances man's life becomes a life–long obsession with the object of love (*heromenon*). The lover seeks to identify himself with the loved to the extent this is humanly possible, for man can never hope to become identical to God. Becoming like God was the original purpose of man's creation, but man forfeited this purpose as a result of his disobedience. However, man is given an opportunity to be restored to his original status with incarnation of God, who is now called to live in Christ.[87] Furthermore, Clement as observed does not consider passions as congenital to man (*ou phusis*, Paed. 2.84.1), and rejects the views of the Stoics such as Zeno and Chrysippus who perceived them as co-inherent false judgments from which we should rid ourselves. For Clement passions are distortions to which we voluntarily agree.[88] Autarchy as a virtue enumerated by Clement can be best understood in this context, it enhances the effort towards Theosis or perfection.

As Clement writes in The Instructor (*Pedagogus*) Book I, Chapter XII, exhorting us to follow the footsteps of Jesus,

"He makes preparation for a ***self-sufficing*** *mode of life, for simplicity, and for girding up our loins, and for free and unimpeded readiness of our journey; in order to the attainment of an eternity of beatitude, teaching each one of us to be his own storehouse. For He says, Take no anxious thought for tomorrow (Mathew 6:34), meaning that the man who has devoted himself to Christ ought to be* ***sufficient*** *to himself, and servant to himself, and moreover lead a life which provides for each day by itself. For it is not in war, but in peace, that we are trained. War needs great preparation, and luxury craves profusion; but peace and love, simple and quiet sisters, require no arms or excessive preparation. The Word is their sustenance."*[89]

---

87 Peter Karavites, *Evil, Freedom, the Road to Perfection in Clement of Alexandria* (Netherlands: Brill, 1999), 178.

88 Karavites, *Evil, Freedom…*, 176.

89 *"The writings of Clement of Alexandria"*, Vol. I. Translated by William Wilson In *Ante-Nicene Christian Library*, edited by Alexander Roberts and James Donaldson (Edinburgh: T & T Clark, 1869), 182.

Being in communion with God through his Son is the path to tread towards autarchy and ultimately journeying into Theosis. Clement enumerates that the virtue of autarchy is one of Divine providence and Grace. One who is in God rises above mere cravings of wants and feels **'no want', - a state of autarchy**. He writes, "For he who has the almighty God, the Word **is in want of nothing**, and never is in straits for what he need...The good man, then, can never be in difficulties so long as he keeps intact his confession towards God. For it appertains to him to ask and to receive whatever he requires from the Father of all; and enjoy what is his own, if he keep the Son. And this also appertains to him, **to feel no want**" (The Instructor, Book III, Chap. VII, *Frugality a good provision for the Christian*) [90] The end of piety as enumerated by Clement is (Book III, *The Instructor*, chapter VII) "...the privilege of wanting nothing. He that has this wealth shall inherit the kingdom of God."[91]

2.5.2 The Attainment of Likeness

For Clement Likeness to God meant living according to virtue. Clement suggests this 'by practicing self-restraint and endurance, by living righteously, by ruling over the passions, by sharing his possessions as far as possible, and by doing good in both word and deed' (*Strom. 2.97.1*). Christian Gnostic became like God by imitating his freedom from passions, self sufficiency and beneficence. He also imitated God's kingly rule, reigning over both the exterior and the interior worlds- 'the wild beasts without and the wild passions within' (*Strom. 6.115.2*).[92]

Clement exhorts the strides in the path to divinization with philosophical parallels drawn from the Old Testament, Plato, Socrates, and Stoics etc. in, *The Stromata* (Book V, Chapter Xiv – Greek Plagiarism From The Hebrews),

"Wherefore also man is said "to have been made in [God's] image and likeness." For the image of God is the divine and royal

90 *"The writings of Clement of Alexandria"*, Vol. I. Translated by William Wilson..., 302-303.

91 *"The writings of Clement of Alexandria"*, Vol. I. Translated by William Wilson..., 303.

92 Russell, *The Doctrine of Deification in the Greek Patristic Tradition...*, 135.

Word, the impassible man; and the image of the image is the human mind. And if you wish to apprehend the likeness by another name, you will find it named in Moses, a divine correspondence. For he says, "Walk after the Lord your God, and keep His commandments." And I reckon all the virtuous, servants and followers of God. Hence, as the Stoics say that the end of philosophy is to live agreeable to nature; and Plato, likeness to God, as we have shown in the second Miscellany. And Zeno the Stoic, borrowing from Plato, and he from the Barbarian philosophy, says that all the good are friends of one another. For Socrates says in the Phoedrus, "that it has not been ordained that the bad should be a friend to the bad, nor the good be not a friend to the good;" as also he showed sufficiently in the Lysis, that friendship is never preserved in wickedness and vice.[93] And then quickly the Athenian stranger similarly says, "that there is conduct pleasing and conformable to God, based on one ancient ground-principle, That like loves like, provided it be within measure. But things beyond measure are congenial neither to what is within nor what is beyond measure. Now it is the case that God is the measure to us of all things." Then proceeding, Plato adds: "For every good man is like every other good man; and so being like to God, he is liked by every good man and by God." At this point I have just recollected the following. In the end of the Timoeus he says: "You must necessarily assimilate that which perceives to that which is perceived, according to its original nature; and it is by so assimilating it that you attain to the end of the highest life proposed by the gods to men, for the present or the future time." For those have equal power with these. He, who seeks, will not stop till he find; and having found, he will wonder; and wondering, he will reign; and reigning, he will rest. And what? Were not also those expressions of Thales derived from these? The fact that God is glorified forever, and that He is expressly called by us the Searcher of hearts, he interprets. For Thales being asked, What is the divinity? said, What has neither beginning nor end."[94]

93 *"The writings of Clement of Alexandria",* Vol. I. Translated by William Wilson ..., 277-278.

94 *"The writings of Clement of Alexandria",* Vol. I. Translated by William Wilson ..., 278.

Furthermore, it is to be noted that for Clement the ideal man, freedom from passions, *autarkia*, *apatheia*, are all primarily a divine attributes. Clement explains that only Christ, as the incarnate divine Logos, is 'absolutely without passion' (άπαξαπλώς (Strom. 6. 9. 71). In attaining *apatheia* the perfect Christian becomes godlike in his freedom from all needs and desires (Strom. 6.71-71), even to the point of not desiring, as his principle goal, his own salvation (Strom. 4.135-6). This is a condition brought about fundamentally by the operation of Grace. Clement conceived both *Apatheia*, and *Autarchy* as divine gifts, differing both from the Stoic *apatheia* (arising simply from the use of right reason), and the Platonic *metriopatheia* (the result of restraining the passions), revealing a profound debt to Philo.[95]

To sum up, as Clement wrote, (Book III, The Instructor, Chapter I):

"*It is then, as appears, the greatest of all lessons to know one's self. For if one knows God; and knowing God, he will be made like God, not by wearing gold or long robes, but by well-doing, and requiring as few things as possible.*"[96] What is sought for is a knowing of self, which should be mistaken for devoid of God, rather realization as profound as found in the Indian Upanashidic tradition, "*Aham Brhamasmi*" Iam Brahman (*Brihadaranyaka* Upanishads 1.4.10). Again, a profound realization state where, "The self (the Soul) is Brahman", "*ayam atma brahma*" (*Brih.* 4.4.5).

2.5.3 Christian Perfection: In God

Clement elucidates through his writings that only God's goodness is perfect and complete. Clement notes the goodness in God, He alone is wholly good. No man except the God-man has ever possessed perfection in all things at once. Men are perfect perhaps in piety or in patience or in other things. 'But I do not know of any man who has been perfect in all ways at once, while he was still a man, except him alone who for our sakes clothed himself with humanity.'[97]

95 Russell, *The Doctrine of Deification in the Greek Patristic Tradition*..., 135.

96 "*The writings of Clement of Alexandria*", Vol. I. Translated by William Wilson..., 273.

97 *Stromata*. IV, 130; II, 305, 21.

The Christian perfection is clearly defined by Clement as he specifies, the perfection to which our Lord calls us does not amount to complete similarity to God. We are to be perfect as our Father by forgiving sins and injuries and living in *apatheia*. A doctor, a philosopher, a gnostic may be called perfect, but none of these, however great, is to be accepted as likeness to God. (*Strom. VII, 88; III, 63, 9).* The teaching of the Stoics that virtue is the same in man and God is emphatically rejected. No one has the power or ability to become perfect as God is *(Ibid. III, 63, 10. Cf. also Strom. II, 135; II, 188, 1 and Strom. VI, 114; II, 489, 17*). The perfection which God asks for us is obedience to the Gospel and life which is above reproach (*Strom*. VII, 88; III, 63, 13).

The Christian perfection is a yearning for perfection in Christ (God) himself, the only perfect. In Him is the Ultimate goodness and perfection; however we traverse and stretch our possibilities to His possibility.

2.6 Social Sensitivity: An Essential Requisite

Towards the late 2nd century Egypt (Alexandria) the rising inflation, high cost of living, and increased taxes placed great burdens not only on the poor but also on the comparatively well-to-do middle class, which finally ruined. Also, the probability of the Church coming into close contact with the cultured and well-to-do classes earlier at Alexandria than elsewhere may have catalyzed the discourse.[98] From the tone of Clement's writings such as *Paedagogus*, one can conclude that the majority of his audience came from Alexandrian middle and upper classes. The problem of wealth was ever disturbing to the pietistic Christians, as in for many great men like St. Antony, who interpreted literally the command of Christ to the rich young man who wanted to be saved, "sell what you have and give to the poor."[99] In response to the literal interpretation, Clement wrote *The Salvation of Rich Man*,[100] in which he stated that wealth is a neutral factor

98 G. W. Butterworth, *Clement of Alexandria* (London: Harvard University Press, 1919), 265.

99 Mt.19:21.

100 Believed to be the only complete example left to us of Clement's popular teaching.

and requires a person to strip the soul of its passions.[101] Possessions are to be regarded as instruments to be used either for good or for evil. Riches/wealth are neutral, instruments to be used for the good of others, 'for welfare of men'[102] "The Word does not command us to renounce property but to manage property without inordinate affection" (*Eclogae Propheticae*).[103] In the matter of almsgiving, Clement's views are varying. On the one hand, he advised that the Christian should not judge who is worthy or unworthy of receiving alms by being niggardly and pretending to test whether or not a person deserves. On the other hand, he stated that alms should be dispensed with discernment to the deserving, for freeloaders, who are lazy and have some possessions, take what can be given to the needy.[104]

Few other documents give us as much detail of the social life of Alexandria in the second century such as the *Paedagogus* or *Instructor*. In the second and third books, a Christian is guided to the appropriate conduct in almost every minute aspect of life: Clement calls especially for the virtue of moderation in the face of luxury, 'which has dearanged all things, it has disgraced man (*Paed.* Book III, 3).[105] Drinking and eating should be in moderation. Drunkenness distorts the senses, and gluttony turns men into pigs and dogs. Servants should not be whistled at, and there should be no spitting, clearing of throats or blowing of noses in public. Sneezing and belching should not produce explosions, but should be suppressed. Food is to be simple and concocted not for pleasure but for nourishment. Clement writes that, food should be, '- as ministering to life, not

101 G.W. Butterworth, *Clement of Alexandria* (London: Harvard University Press, 1919), 291.

102 Ibid., 299.

103 *Clement of Alexandria's Eclogae Propheticae* (or Extracts), found in the form of notes.

104 http://www.britannica.com/biography/Saint-Clement-of-Alexandria (28/11/2015).

105 *"The writings of Clement of Alexandria"*, Vol. I. Translated by William Wilson, In *Ante-Nicene Christian Library*, edited by Alexander Roberts and James Donaldson (Edinburgh: T & T Clark, 1869), 288.

to luxury' (*Paed.* Book II, Chap. I).[106] Bathing should be done with modesty and never for pleasure. Too much bathing causes weakness and dizziness. The kiss of peace can be a dangerous thing, and an unholy kiss is poisonous and fraudulent; it is no proof of love (*Paed.* Book III, Chapter XI).[107] Clement staunchly criticized excessive fondness for jewels and gold ornaments, 'And it is monstrous for one to live in luxury, while many are in want. How much more glorious is it to do good to many, than to live sumptuously! How much wiser to spend money on human beings, than on jewels and gold.' (Book III, Chap. XIII)[108] Wine is especially dangerous for the young, since it adds fire to fire, joining the burning years of life to the fiery liquid of wine (Paed. Book II, Chap. II).[109]

Clement draws much of ethical material from Musonius Rufus[110] and while his precepts for moderation are found elsewhere (as even in Buddhist Philosophy to which detailed discussion is being made in the following chapter), the variety and detail of his account are his own. While some other writers recognized the need for a regimen which covers all human behavior, no one in antiquity achieved this aim as completely as Clement did. Clement's comprehensive instruction is striking; however, the question arises as to its prominence in whole of his thought. Is this just an elementary instruction on proper behavior to Christian pupils preparing for higher learning, or is he permeating this extraordinary mass of details with the fundamental principles of his thought? The majority readers of the *Paedagogus* would find the instructions as, amusement and even express bewilderment at the details which Clement regards as necessary for the Christian life; Certainly, it isn't product of a random

106 *"The writings of Clement of Alexandria"*, Vol. I. Translated by William Wilson..., 187.

107 *"The writings of Clement of Alexandria"*, Vol. I. Translated by William Wilson, 330.

108 *"The writings of Clement of Alexandria"*, Vol. I. Translated by William Wilson..., 268.

109 *"The writings of Clement of Alexandria"*, Vol. I. Translated by William Wilson..., 201.

110 Gaius Musonius Rufus was a Roman Stoic philosopher of the 1st century AD.

discourse rather it renders fertility to cultivating right dispositions and qualities, with setting out Christian duties to praxis.[111]

Conclusion

As rightly put by Eric Osborn in *Clement of Alexandria*, the final goal of ethics for clement is assimilation to God, includes freedom from passions, as well as steadfastness, purity, contemplation, faith, love, searching for God, separation from sensible things and communion with intellectual realities, gentleness, benevolence, piety, a forgiving spirit, kindness, self-sufficiency, and the imitation of Christ.[112]

This research tries to explore *autarchy* as a modest self sufficiency of man, characterized by the consumption only of necessary goods. This self sufficiency in Clement prepares a theological premise and journeys into the realm of *Theosis* also connecting it. Relevantly, the need to become self sufficient has certainly to do immensely with the contemporary economic, ecological and social crisis around the globe and particularly India. The far spread poverty, the consumerist attitude in consumption of goods, the large gap between the haves and have-nots all raise alarms for Indian economy in context of global financial crisis and recessions. The need to become self-sufficient has certainly to do with the current global economic, ecological and energy crisis. Around the Globe, nations are bewildered and discussing means to minimize any avoidable future loss. Clement of Alexandria in the 2nd century had envisioned a new social order based upon the Self-Sufficiency, simplicity, sharing of wealth and resources rather than competition and private ownership, that holds true for present-day global socio-economic context.

---

111 Eric Osborn, *Clement of Alexandria* (U.K: Cambridge University Press, 2005), 242.

112 Osborn, *Clement of Alexandria*..., 240.

Chapter 3

Greed Line and *Autarchy* in Indian Thought

3.1 Introduction

The Indian context of far spread socio-economic inequalities and alarming problem of poverty, have all directed our minds towards better structural policies and alternate holistic solutions. The alarming statistics/reports echo the need for better efforts in eradicating poverty and economic disparities. With high incidence of poverty, Income disparity, Unemployment etc. the Indian economic future remains in shackles. A Critical introspection as, Urga Mohan Jha remarks in preface to, *Rural Development In India*, Governmental Poverty alleviation programs, Poverty eradication programmes, self-employment schemes were ill-conceived and clumsily implemented.[113] Development strategies should incorporate greater involvements of advisory groups from ethical and moral structural categories, as well as academic and policy circles.

The World Council of Churches and its Advisory group on economic matters have played prominent role in working closely with and calling upon Churches, governments, and international institutions to respond justly and sustainably to the global crisis. As

113 Urga Mohan Jha, ed., *Rural Development in India* (New Delhi: Anmol Publications, 1995), 4.

the Central committee Statement on Just finance and Economy of life notes, "...The financial system of recent times has shaped the world more than ever before. However, by becoming the engine of virtual growth and wealth, it has enriched some people but has harmed many more, creating poverty, unemployment, hunger and death; widening the gap between rich and the poor; marginalizing certain groups of people; eroding the whole meaning of human life..."[114]

3.2 The Global Crisis

Despite enormous progress, and globalization projects even today, about 800 million people still live in extreme poverty and suffer from hunger. Over 160 million children under age five have inadequate height for their age due to insufficient food. Currently, 57 million children of primary school age are not in school. Almost half of global workers are still working in vulnerable conditions, rarely enjoying the benefits associated with decent work. About 16,000 children die each day before celebrating their fifth birthday, mostly from preventable causes. The maternal mortality ratio in the developing regions is 14 times higher than in the developed regions. Just half of pregnant women in the developing regions receive the recommended minimum of four antenatal care visits.

The global financial crisis of 2008-2009, which brought the global economy precariously close to collapse and which continues to erode livelihoods and impoverish millions of people, turned the spotlight, if only for a brief period, on the role of greed in generating and concentrating wealth and on the heavy costs of greed on society as a whole. At the height of the crisis, the United Nations (UNCTAD 2009) made the following observation:

"No doubt, without [the] greed of too many agents trying to squeeze double-digit returns out of an economic system that grows only in the lower single-digit range, the crisis would not have erupted with such force."[115]

---

114 Pamela Brubaker and Rogate Mshana ,eds., *Justice not Greed* (Geneva: WCC Publication, 2010), 219.

115 Athena Peralta & Rogate R. Mshana, eds., *The Greed Line* (Geneva: WCC Publications, 2014), 1.

3.3 Poverty, Wealth and Ecology Project of the WCC

World Council of Churches has extended discussions focusing on poverty, wealth and ecology since its 8th Assembly at Harare, 1998 directly with AGAPE (Alternative Globalization Addressing People and Earth) process. Also, the WCC's motto of preferential option for people in poverty remains relevant today.[116]

The Poverty, Wealth and Ecology Project of the WCC addresses the vital issues of our times – unbridled greed, deepening poverty and socio-economic inequality and widespread ecological destruction – based on the recognition that poverty and wealth are two sides of the same coin: in order to fight poverty and ecological degradation, the reverse side, i.e. excessive wealth, also has to be dealt with (Mshana 2007). Wealth has to be addressed alongside poverty for a number of reasons:

"They have common causes and integrally related characteristics: the ability of the rich to earn a living for example is the inability of the poor; the strength of the rich is the weakness of the poor. Worse still, excessive wealth is itself a cause of poverty. The drive to create a rising tide of wealth and become rich does not benefit rich and poor alike such that 'all boats rise.' It does not bring an end to poverty but often exacerbates it. And by concentrating only on poverty, attention is deflected from the rich. At most they are seen as the possible source of a solution to poverty. They are not seen as a major part of the problem" (Taylor, ed. 2003).

WCC-commissioned studies on the links between poverty, wealth and ecology conducted in Africa (Mshana, ed. 2012,), Asia (Peralta, ed. 2010), Latin America and the Caribbean (Mshana, ed. 2009), Europe (Pavlovic, ed. 2011) and North America (Kennedy, ed. 2012) provide evidence that wealth creation and accumulation have often taken place to the detriment of people's wellbeing and the health of ecosystems. The findings of these studies help to bolster Harry De Lange and Bob Goudzwaard's (1995) argument, in *Beyond Poverty and Affluence: Toward and economy of care*, that:

116 Athena Peralta & Rogate R. Mshana, eds., *Linking Poverty Wealth and Ecology* (Geneva: WCC Publications, 2013), vii.

"Only by defining the upper limits of consumption and thus of income for the rich can the real needs of the poor be satisfied and the impact of the economy on the environment be brought under control."

It was, however, the APRODEV study project on *Christianity, Poverty and Wealth* (Taylor, ed. 2003) that first articulated the proposal to develop so-called **wealth or greed lines** to stand in counterpart to poverty lines:

"Can excessive wealth be defined as concretely as we sometimes define poverty? Is there a wealth line above which no one should rise just as there is a poverty line below which no one should be allowed to fall? Can we speak of 'relative wealth' in the way we speak of 'relative poverty' so focusing once again on the unacceptable disparities within communities and countries, rich or poor, as well as between them? What might be the indicators of excessive wealth to stand alongside poverty indicators...?"

Reacting to these urgent challenges, the WCC, through the Poverty, Wealth and Ecology Project, convened the Greed Line Study Group in 2009, composed of multidisciplinary experts, with the following mandate:

- to establish how greed could be measured and monitored;
- to analyze how to avert greed in production and consumption;
- to work out theological, economic, ethical and moral guidelines for just and sustainable production and consumption; and
- to propose how greed/wealth lines could contribute towards building alternatives to the current economic system that has proved to be both inequitable and unsustainable.

3.4 Greed Line

In Greek, the word 'greedy' is '*aplistos*', which is derived from the privative '*a*' and '*plistos*' meaning complete' or full. Therefore being 'greedy' is having insatiable or unfulfilled desires. In the same vein, also interesting is to recollect the economic standard that *wants are unlimited*. However, there is a need for strong ethical and moral economic outlook to control the deepening slit created by uncontrolled consumption.

The Report of the Greed Line Study Group of the World Council of Churches (WCC) explains the basic approaches briefly as, "The development of a greed line is aimed at bringing attention to the point where wealth and wealth accumulation have harmful consequences and could be considered as greed." Bob Goudzwaard (2011, unpublished) points out that such a line has to be founded on well-defined social and ecological criteria to avoid accusations of subjectivity and moralism. It must be clear with regard to who we are speaking to as well as cognizant of data limitations. He identifies three impulses which could, to some extent, be combined: the natural law or human rights approach, the enrichment approach, and the carrying capacity approach.[117]

The basic principle of equal access by all human beings to the Earth's fruits is the rationale behind the natural law approach and international treaties such as the UN Declaration of Human Rights. To the extent that such treaties are recognized and legally-binding, it involves an obligation by affluent countries and people to transfer resources to countries and people subsisting on or below the poverty line. Bob Goudzwaard (2011, unpublished) even suggests that:

"Neglecting these economic claims of the poor by the rich can therefore be ethically interpreted as a manifestation of collective greed."[118]

Enrichment is a dynamic approach that shows how wealth generation and accumulation result in impoverishment. While it is not an easy exercise to establish connections – whether direct or indirect – between enrichment and impoverishment, clear examples of victimization are available. For instance, poor countries continue to make net financial transfers to rich countries, in which the net sum of interests and amortization which has to be paid by the former to the latter is higher than the sum of private investments plus development aid received from the latter. This anomaly exposes relations of structural dependency between poor and rich countries that enable enrichment of already rich countries to take place,

117 Athena Peralta & Rogate R. Mshana, eds., *The Greed Line* (Geneva: WCC Publications, 2014), 14.

118 Peralta and Mshana, eds., *The Greed Line...*, 14.

leading to impoverishment of already poor countries, and potentially signifying greed on the side of rich countries.[119]

Finally as noted, the carrying capacity approach is based on the awareness that personal and collective levels of material production and consumption involve an inbuilt claim on the Earth's resources which are governed by regenerative constraints. A good illustration is the calculation of ecological footprints defined as "*the amount of biologically productive land-and sea area which is needed to regenerate the resources which the human population uses for its consumption, and to absorb or render harmless the corresponding waste.*" Linking these calculations to a greed line requires deeper thought. But, as an initial step, calculating ecological footprints at the level of national economies – a task which is already being undertaken – could be seen as the maximum tolerable degree of material consumption per capita on the basis of the criterion of global sustainability."[120]

The Report also categorically presents various models for defining greed line such as:

- ***Defining a wealth/greed line based on percentages above average or median incomes.*** In some countries national poverty lines are determined on the basis of percentages below the average or median household income. In the same vein, a wealth or greed line could be established on the basis of a given percentage above the average or median household income using available statistical evidence about household income and the proportional relationship between minimal and maximum incomes.[121]
- ***Defining a greed line based on an ethical social consumption function and redistribution.***

  Carlos Larrea (2011, 2014 forthcoming) develops the concept of an ethical social consumption function that factors in inequitable socio-economic conditions and ecological limits, and derives the greed line from the

119 Peralta and Mshana, eds., *The Greed Line* ..., 14-15.

120 Peralta and Mshana, eds., *The Greed Line* ..., 14-15.

121 Peralta & Mshana, eds., *The Greed Line*..., 15.

said function. The greed line is defined as "*the maximum ethically acceptable individual consumption in the current global economy, simultaneously characterised by the social exclusion of a large proportion of the world population affected by poverty, a high level of national and international inequality, luxurious consumption accounting for a large share of global output, and the lack of environmental sustainability, affecting the right of future generations to achieve adequate living conditions.*"

- ***Defining a greed line based on an ethical production function***

  To stand alongside the ethical consumption function, an ethical production function could also be formulated to offer guidance on appropriate levels and methods of production, investment and profits in accordance with social and ecological standards. In this regard, Rosario Guzman (2010 in Peralta, ed.) recommends setting production lines (including export and import lines) as well as profit lines that place thresholds on the amount of profits as a percentage of GDP, profits from investments, and interest on debt. The major difficulty, however, lies in determining where exactly to draw the lines. The social and ecological bases for setting production and profit lines need to be objectively elaborated.[122]

3.5 A Framework: Towards Multidimensional Greed Indicators

The WCC report also makes strong suggestions for developing indicators which could alert policy makers and the general public to critical manifestations of greed. These could also inform implementation of policies and measures to avert greed and plan equitable and sustainable production, consumption and distribution. The indicators should clearly expose the economic, socio-political and ecological consequences of greed as well as allow quantitative assessment using either a linear scale or a positive-negative alternative.

122 Athena Peralta and Rogate R. Mshana, eds., *The Greed Line* (Geneva: WCC Publications, 2014), 14-17.

Weights could also be assigned to every indicator towards developing an index that allows for a ranking of countries.

As a counterpart to the multidimensional poverty indicators first developed by the University of Oxford's Poverty and Human Development Initiative, Michael Taylor proposes the development of multidimensional greed indicators (MGIs) that take into consideration the more obvious economic as well as the non-economic dimensions of greed. Specifically, the indicators could look at categories of health, education, empowerment, relationships, environment and security and, in each case, would refer to the potential greed of an individual and its consequences for others.[123]

3.6 Indian Economic Context

For India enormous social sensitivity and philanthropic fervor is knit in its socio-cultural and economic fabric. Remarkably, the moral, ethical and Socio-economic view in Gandhian thought is a significant milieu for Indian context. However, the present Indian context of far-flung economic disparities, poverty issues raises alarms to a social sensitivity and ethical concern. One in three of the world's poorest people are living in India, the world's second-fastest growing economy, according to a new study by the World Bank.[124]

About 30 crore people still live in extreme poverty in India even as the Millennium Development Goal (MGD) programme will expire in December, as per reports of United Nations. India, adopted the United Nation's MGD in 2000 with an aim to free millions from extreme poverty, hunger, illiteracy and poor health.[125] These above stated conditions however do not override the fact of development and eradication of poverty achieved by India as a nation.

---

123 Peralta & Mshana, eds., *The Greed Line...*, 17.

124 http://www.telegraph.co.uk/news/worldnews/asia/india/10003228/India-has-one-third-of-worlds-poorest-says-World-Bank.html (12/08/2015).

125 http://timesofindia.indiatimes.com/india/30-crore-people-still-live-in-extreme-poverty-in-India-UN-report/articleshow/46122767.cms (12/08/2015).

3.7 Indian Philosophical Wealth

The Indian Philosophical wealth is at instances undermined and this self affliction comes as a perfect example of idioms such as poor man in rags sitting on a heap of treasures or monkey who cast away the precious jewel into the river. Dr. Paulos Mar Gregorios discusses this in his paper *On Poverty of Philosophy and Philosophy of Poverty: The Task of Indian Philosophy Today.* Furthermore, with discontentment for both imageries, he concludes saying, "The treasure is there; the monkey has cast it in a place in the river from which it can be recovered. To recover it the will must be quickened, the skills need to be resharpened; and a new social and personal discipline of acquiring *amalaprajna*[126] for the philosopher, and a social discipline of greater justice, there can be no true philosophy. A tall order-but not too tall for the invincible spirit of Indian humanity.[127]

Construing the Indian Philosophical precepts provides a wealth of thoughts into the concept of *Autarkia*, as a mode envisaged in various categories. In the Introduction to Indian Philosophy, Sarvepalli Radhakrishnan explains the *Samkaras* commentary on the first Sutra of the *Vedanta Sutras*, about the four conditions essential for any student of philosophy. "He must stand outside of life and look on it". So, it is said that he must have no love of the present or the future. Only then can he stake his all on clear thinking and honest judgement and develop an impersonal cosmic outlook with devotedness to fact. To get this temper he must suffer a change of heart, which is insisted on in the third condition, where the student is enjoined to acquire tranquility, self-restraint, renunciation, patience, peace of mind and faith.[128] The etymological meaning of economy (*oikos+nomos*-management of the household) must be interpreted in a wider ecumenical world in which a creative dialogue among God, humans and world is sustained and promoted.

126 Pure Wisdom (as in Buddhism).

127 K. M. George, ed., *Philosophy East and West* (Kottayam: Mar Gregorios Foundation, 2013), 407-408.

128 Sarvepalli Radhakrishnan, *Indian Philosophy, Vol. I* (New Delhi: Oxford University Press, 1999), 20.

3.7.1 Principle Thoughts

Among the varied Indian philosophical interpretations conveying the meaning of Self-sufficiency more precisely are some terms, such as these:

3.7.1.1 *Purna*

Explicating the meaning of the complex word *Purna*, *Pr*-from which the word purna is formed to denote sustenance, fullness, self-sufficiency, self-containedness are carried throughout the Indian tradition, overlooking the meaning as water or element (*bhuta*) recorded in the *Nighantu-Nirukta*.[129] In some Buddhist texts, however, the word *purna* is also used as noun to signify 'a monk', implying the idea 'fullness', self-sufficiency', perfection'. The basic meanings that can be gleaned from various usages can be stated as fullness, self-sufficiency, perfection.[130] The celebrated Purnamantra or the shanti mantra of Isha Upanishad which forms a part of the Shukla Yajurveda[131] profoundly enumerates the purna (completeness) which is intrinsically related to the Ultimate. The verses,

"Completeness is that, completeness is this, from completeness, completeness comes forth. Completeness from completeness taken away, completeness to completeness added, completeness alone remains."

3.7.1.2 Aparigraha

Aparigraha is a compound word in Sanskrit, fused from "*a*" and "*parigrah*". "*A*" as prefix refers "non-" or negation in Sanskrit, and the word *Parigrah* means 'to amass', 'to crave', 'to seek', 'to receive or accept'. The word includes in its scope outer worldly possessions as well as inner attachment to material rewards, rather than doing the

---

129 The Nighantu and the Nirukta, is the oldest Indian treatise on etymology, philology and semantics.
https://archive.org/details/nighantuniruktao00yaskuoft (10/1/16).

130 Bettina Baumer, ed., *Kalatattvakosa, Vol. II* (New Delhi: Indira Gandhi National Centre for the Arts, 2003), 430.

131 Ashim Kumar Bhattacharya, *Hindu Dharma* (New York: IUniverse, Inc., 2006), 86.

right thing or good because it is the right thing or good. *Parigraha* thus includes the consequences as well as the intent; to sum up the meaning encompasses the possessions as well as the craving, a sense of possessiveness and hoarding. Aparigraha has insightful tradition largely in Yoga system of Patanjali as well as forms a sturdy basis in Jainism.

In the *Yoga system of Patanjali,* (Harvard edition) translator James Wood explains, *aparigraha* is the virtue of abstaining from appropriating objects because one understands the disadvantages in "acquiring them, keeping them, losing them, being attached to them, or in harming them."[132] Patanjali suggests that greed and coveting material wealth increases greed and possessiveness, a cycle that distracts from good reasons for activity that should motivate a person, and ultimately to a state where a person seeks material wealth without effort and by harming, hurting or impoverishing someone else, or some living creature. Yoga Sutra's verse 2.39 states,

अपरिग्रहस्थैर्ये जन्मकथंतासंबोधः ॥३९॥. *With constancy of Aparigraha, a spiritual illumination of the how and why of motives and birth emerges. (Patanjali, Yoga Sutra 2.39).*

Self-control from possessiveness and greed, or *Aparigraha,* leads one away from destructive and ruinous greed, refraining from harming others, and towards the spiritual state of virtues activities. The virtue of non-coveting, non-possessing is understood as means of *Sadhana,*[133] path of spiritual existence. In outer world, *aparigraha* manifests as non-possessiveness with simple living; while in psychological terms, it is a state of non-attachment, non-craving and one that envelops the sense of contentment.[134]

Jainism also has *aparigraha* as one of its core values. The three core concepts of Jainism are, non-violence, (*ahimsa*), non possession (*aparigraha*), and nondogmatism (*anekantavada*). *Aparigraha* presents in its insightful thought premise a necessary solution to the problem of human greed, anxiety, consumerism, and wastefulness.

132 Patanjali, *The Yoga System of Patanjali,* translated by James Wood (U.K: Harvard University Press, 2003), 178-182.

133 A spiritual exercise, discipline or exertion undertaken towards pursuit of a specific goal.

134 Patanjali, *The Yoga System of Patanjali,* translated by James Wood..., 183.

This application can be unequivocally prescribed to ethical resource consumption and ecological concerns of the present times.

In addition, the tradition of Jainism gets its name from great spiritual masters called *Jinas*, meaning "conquerors". They have taught that life, in all its myriad expressions (human, animal, insect, plant, water, earth, air, and fire), possesses an eternal quality that is noble and worthy of respect. Each eternal quality embodied in persons, animals, and things is called *jiva*, a perfect entity endowed with a capacity for omniscience and bliss. Also, in Jainism the path to liberation is that of unconditional nonviolence. Any encroachment on the life of another is a form of violence for Jainism. Cruelty and killing of any sort is violence,but so too is desire, lust, and greed.[135]

3.8 Indian Economic Perspectives

The vedic world view presents a positive attitude towards the material world and human life therein. The prayer of the Vedic people is: "*May we live a hundred autumns*". (*jeevema sharatah shatam*), enjoying the fruits of the earth. An ideal human society would be people living in harmony with each other and the elements of nature according to *Rta*. The Vedic and several other scriptures lay emphasis on the economics of sharing. The *Rig veda* emphatically declares, that natures resources are meant to not for a few but for all, it is a person's moral duty to share. According to hymn 10.6 of the Rigveda 'one who eats alone without sharing, is a sinner'(*kevalagho bhavati kevaladi*). The Rig veda again reminds people that everything in this world is filled with God (*Ishavyasam*). And hence even while one enjoys wealth, it must be done with a sense of renunciation; further, one must not appropriate what belongs to others.

The Atharva veda while finding nothing wrong in accumulating wealth asks people to "accumulate with a hundred hands, but distribute with a thousand hands". The concepts of *Yajna* and *Rna* in the Vedas point to a holistic economic morality. Human beings are understood as being born with a debt (*rna*) towards nature and its elements (*bhutas*). *Yajna* which originally meant "offering" is an important means to repay debt. In the *panchamahayajna* humans offer

135 Mark Juergensmeyer and Wade Clark Roof, ed., *Encyclopedia of Global Religions* (London: Sage Publications, 2012), 607.

the cosmos and elements of nature to God and thereby affirm their interrelationship with the material world and with God. Bhagvad Gita 3:13, repeats the Rigvedic idea in a more illustrated manner "*evil are they and evil do they eat who cook only for themselves.*[136]

3.9 Buddhism: The Philosophical Aspiration

Buddhism has indeed been a great source of Philosophical wealth across the world. Many philosophical deliberations of West find its roots in Buddhist thought, celebrated Philosophers of Greece have posthumously acknowledged their foreknowledge of Indian and Buddhist thought. This holds true in case of Clement of Alexandria; one can easily trace of his encounters with Buddhist and Indian Philosophy, even though a probable naïve exposure or familiarity. Clement's knowledge of Indian religion, shown by his numerous rather critical references to Indian customs and the correct distinction he made between the *Brahmins* and *Sarmanians* may be more relevant to his outlook than is sometimes admitted. The early Third century saw strong links being made between the Roman Empire and India and these links affected thought as well as the trade.[137]

Clement of Alexandria quotes of in The *Miscellanies* Book I, Chapter XV, "Some, too, of the Indians obey the precepts of Buddha; whom, on account of his extraordinary sanctity, they have raised to divine honors." Clement also notes, the writing of Megasthenes, the contemporary of Seleucus Nicanor, writes as follows in the third of his books, on *Indian affairs*: "All that was said about nature by the ancients is said also by those who philosophize beyond Greece: some things by the Brahmins among the Indians, and others by those called Jews in Syria."[138]

Furthermore, Clement speaks highly of Egyptian and Indian Gymnosophists (Chapter IV, *Miscellanies*, Book VI), "The

136 Jacob Parapally and Antony Kalliath, eds., *Theology of Economics in the Globalized World Indian Approaches* (Bangalore: Indian Theological Association and Asian Trading Corporation, 2010), 205.

137 Frend, *The Rise of Christianity…*, 372.

138 William Wilson, trans. and eds., *The Writings of Clement of Alexandria*, Vol. I of *Ante Nicene Christian Library*, edited by Alexander Roberts and James Donaldson (Edinburgh: T & T Clark), 399.

Philosophy of the Indians, too, has been celebrated". And goes on to narrate the story of Alexander of Macedonia taking captive "ten Indian Gymnosophists that seemed the best and most sententious, proposed to them problems,..."[139]

3.9.1 Buddhism: The Greaco-Indian Connect

The interaction between Hellenistic Greece and Buddhism is believed to have started when Alexander the Great conquered the Achaemenid Empire[140] and further regions of Central Asia in 334 BCE, crossing the Indus and Jhelum rivers, and going as far as the Beas, thus establishing direct contact with India, the birthplace of Buddhism. Moreover, Alexander established several cities in his new territories in the areas of the Oxus and Bactria, and Greek settlements further advanced to the Khyber Pass, Gandhara (*Taxila*) and the Punjab. These regions correspond to an exclusive geographical gateway between the Himalayas and the Kush mountains, through which largely interaction between India and Central Asia took place, creating powerful trade and cultural exchange.

Following Alexander's death on June 10, 323 BCE, the *Diadochoi* (successors) founded their own kingdoms in Asia Minor and Central Asia. General Seleucus set up the Seleucid Kingdom, which extended as far as India. Later, the Eastern part of the Seleucid Kingdom broke away to form the Greco-Bactrian Kingdom (3rd-2nd century BCE), followed by the Indo-Greek Kingdom (2nd–1st century BCE), and later the Kushan Empire (1st-3rd century CE). The interaction of Greek and Buddhist cultures operated over several centuries until it ended in the 5th century CE with the invasions of the White Huns, and later the expansion of Islam.[141]

And this close association between Greeks and Buddhism probably led to exchanges on the philosophical plane as well. Many of the early Mahayana theories of reality and knowledge can be correlated to Greek philosophical schools of thought. Mahayana Buddhism has

139 William Wilson, trans. and ed., *The Writings of Clement of Alexandria...*, 324.

140 The Achaemenid Empire, also called the First Persian Empire, was an empire based in Western Asia, founded by Cyrus the Great, around 550 BCE.

141 http://www.cs.mcgill.ca/~rwest/link-suggestion/wpcd_2008-09_augmented/wp/g/Greco-Buddhism.htm (10/1/2016).

been described as the form of Buddhism which, (regardless of how its later forms became effected by popular religious thoughts) seems to have originated in the Greco-Buddhist communities of India, through a conflation of the Greek Democritean-Sophistic-Skeptical tradition with the rudimentary and unformalized empirical and skeptical elements already present in early Buddhism. For e.g. cynics denied the relevancy of human conventions and opinions (described as *typhos*, literally "smoke" a metaphor for "illusion" or "error"), including verbal expressions, in favor of the raw experience of reality. They stressed the independence from externals to achieve happiness: "Happiness is not pleasure, for which we need external, but virtue, which is complete without external" (3rd *epistole* of Crates). Similarly the Prajnaparamita, precursor of the Madhyamika, explained that all things are like foam, or bubbles, "empty, false, and fleeting," and that "only the negation of all views can lead to enlightenment." In order to evade the world of illusion, the Cynics recommended the discipline and struggle ("*askisis kai machi*") of philosophy, the practice of "*autarkia*" (self-rule), and a lifestyle exemplified by Diogenes/ Stoics, which, like Buddhist monks, renounced earthly possessions. These conceptions, in combination with the idea of "*philanthropia*" (universal loving kindness), are strikingly reminiscent of Buddhist *Prajna* (wisdom) and *Karuna* (compassion).[142]

The destruction of ignorance and cravings is the way to attain the ultimate goal of Buddhism. Human suffering is due to the presence of a triad consists of *lobha* (greed), *dosa* (hatred) and *moha* (delusion). According to Buddhism, the evil mental traits that cause human suffering function concomitantly at the two main levels of the human psyche. At the emotional level are *lobha* and *dosa* and at cognitive level is *moha*. All human suffering, whether it is at the individual level, or at the societal level is a consequence of these three psychological traits. An enlightened one is a person who completely eliminates these traits and such a person is regarded as one who has attained *Nibbana,* in *The Ultimate Goal of Buddhism and the Doctrine of No-Self By P.D Premasiri.* He also points that Buddhism, "They present a specific world-view, an account of the

142 http://diatribe-column.blogspot.in/2008/03/greek-buddha-where-east-meets-west.html (10/01/2016).

human predicament as well as a spiritual goal for man conceived as liberation or salvation. The attainment of this goal is believed to be a consequence of a systematic transformation of the person by means of a graduated path of moral training and perfection (as in the Theocentric view of Buddhism, exceptions apply such as *Pali* canonical tradition, which is largely non-theistic)[143] It is pivotal also to notice the Buddhist notion of seeking a path of moderation between two extremes, or feeling satisfied with what they have and not feeling that resources are never sufficient to meet increasing desires. However, globalization and capitalism has influenced this phenomenon of increasing desires to untamed limits, exploiting the resources and consuming greedily.

In the same context, very appealing is the case study of Thailand as found in the excerpts from a paper of Institute for Population and Social Research, Mahidol University, Thailand, *'Generally, it can be claimed that feeling self-sufficient may be influenced by the Buddhist philosophy that the path to happiness lies in training one's mind not to crave things without limit and so to avoid unreasonably torturing oneself. "Feeling satisfied with what one has" is a phrase that the Thais hear throughout their lives.'*

(Paper written for the international conference on "**Happiness and Public Policy**" organized by the Public Policy Development Office (PPDO), the Government House, Bangkok and the United Nations Economic and Social Commission for Asia and the Pacific (UNESCAP), on 18-19 July 2007 at the United Convention Center (UNCC) in Bangkok, Thailand.).[144] The predominance of Thevarada[145] Buddhism is considered an important aspect of the Thai setting since it influences Thai people's attitudes, thoughts, and way of life. Inspired by Buddhism, Thai lay people tend to subscribe to the Buddhist notion of seeking a path of moderation between two

143 Robert E. Carter, ed., *God the Self and Nothingness* (New York: Paragon House, 1990), 26.

144 http://www.happysociety.org/ppdoconference/session_papers/session17/session17_rossarin.pdf (11/01/2016).

145 Theravada, 'the Doctrine of the Elders', is the school of Buddhism that draws its scriptural inspiration from the Tipitaka, or Pali canon, which scholars generally agree contains the earliest surviving record of the Buddha's teachings.

extremes, feeling satisfied with what they have and not feeling that resources are never sufficient to meet increasing desires. However, globalization and capitalism may have influenced this phenomenon of increasing desires.[146]

3.10 Gandhian Thought

Gandhian socio-economic thought serves as a platter for analyzing Indian context. The widespread economic and social disparities condole as perils of unprecedented Globalization. Gandhian thought offers a wide set of alternatives to the crisis global economies face today; *Sarvodaya*, *Ramarajya* (kingdom of love, Justice and Righteousness), *Asteya* (Non-stealing), *Aparigraha* (Renunciation), *Ahimsa* (Non-injury) are some pivotal features. The Gandhian frame of reference is largely inherited from the Upanishidic-Gita tradition and notion of *Atman* as its centre.[147] Furthermore, the Gandhian economic philosophy like his political, social and religious philosophy is based on *Satyagraha*[148] and *Ahimsa*.[149] Albert Schweitzer[150] and several other Christian interpreters of Gandhian thought consider the emphasis on social service to be indicative of Christian influence on Gandhi.[151]

3.10.1 Selected Gandhian Economic and Ethical Features

Gandhian economic and ethical features readily provide a hybrid resolution for Indian context. As J.C Kumarappa remarks, "there is no such thing as the principles of Economics of Gandhiji. With Gandhiji economics is a part of a way of life...Only two life principles govern all Gandhiji's economic, social, political and other considerations, viz. Truth and Non-violence."[152]

146 http://www.happysociety.org/ppdoconference/session_papers/session17/session17_rossarin.pdf (11/01/2016).

147 V. T. Patil, ed., *Studies on Gandhi* (New Delhi: Sterling Publishers, 1983), 5.

148 Insistence on Truth.

149 Non-violence, Love.

150 J. S. Mathur, ed., *Gandhian Thought and Contemporary Society* (Bombay: Bhartiya Vidya Bhavan, 1974), 255.

151 T. S. Devadoss, *Sarvodaya* (Madras: University of Madras, 1974), 83.

152 J. C. Kumarappa, *Gandhian Economic Thought* (Varanasi: Sarva Seva Sangh Prakashan, 1951), 5.

3.10.1.1 *Non-stealing*

According to Gandhi it is theft (1) to take anything belonging to another without his permission, even if it be with his knowledge; (2) to take something in the belief that it is nobody's property, for e.g things found on the roadside; (3) to take something from another even with his permission if we have no real need of it; (4) to improperly multiply our wants; (5) to desire acquisition of anything belonging to others.[153] What is most significant and what lends an added contemporary relevance to Gandhi's exegesis of the age-old ethical principle of non-stealing is that he related it to life-styles and the consequent grinding poverty affecting millions of people all over the world. One is reminded of Emile Zola's deeply disturbing comment: "behind every great fortune is a crime."[154]

3.10.1.2 Non-Possession

As Prof. M.P Mathai remarks (*Mahatma Gandhi's world View*), "For Gandhi, possession of superfluous things was a crime against God and Humanity. If each retained possession only of what he needed, no one could be in want, and all would be in contentment." In the contemporary world-experience of resource depletion, drying up of sources of energy and other related ecological problems the vow of non-possession, though seemingly impossible and subjective must be kept constantly in view and in its light our possession must be critically re-examined and reduced progressively and voluntarily.[155]

3.10.1.3 *Yajna* or Sacrifice

According to Gandhi, "*Yajna* means an act directed towards the welfare of others, done without desiring any return for it whether of a temporal or spiritual nature. An 'act' here must be taken in its widest sense, and includes thought and word, as well as deed, 'others' embraces not only humanity but all life."[156] Gandhi said: "*yajna*,

153 M. P. Mathai, *Mahatma Gandhi's World-View* (New Delhi: Gandhi Peace Foundation, 2000), 131.

154 Mathai, *Mahatama Gandhi's World*..., 132.

155 Mathai, *Mahatma Gandhi's World*..., 132.

156 Mathai, *Mahatma Gandhi's World*..., 144.

having come to us with our birth we are debtors all our lives, and thus for ever bound to serve the universe. And even as a bond slaves receives food, clothing and so on from the master whom he serves, so should we gratefully accept such gifts as may be assigned to us by the Lord of the Universe.

3.10.1.4 Decentralisation

For Gandhi *Khadi* and village industries stood for a decentralized economic system that can promote the economic and moral regeneration of the masses of India.[157] The depiction of Gandhi's ideas on decentralization would be incomplete if it is not mentioned that Gandhian economics is not based entirely on handicrafts and cottage industries. Gandhi was not against large scale industries per se. On the other hand he admitted its due role and significance.

He visualized a balanced and organic relationship between the two sectors. In the Gandhi scheme, "Cottage and large scale industries were not competing alternatives but complementary and helpful to each other. Gandhi wanted small scale production and large industries to be developed in such a way that each sector will provide those supplies which cannot be produced by the other."[158]

3.10.1.5 Doctrine of *Trusteeship*

What is unique about Gandhian economic theory is that Gandhi did not accept the concept of ownership as such whether it be private or state. He considered both as equally exploitive and hence inconsistence with non-violence.[159] M.P Mathai explains that Gandhi advised the owners of property to consider themselves as trustees of the property which really belonged to the whole society and manage it accordingly, taking only what they needed for their own upkeep but using the rest for the welfare of society.[160] The Indian philosophical categories of thought in Gandhi vehemently

157 Mathai, *Mahatma Gandhi's World...*, 193.

158 Mathai, *Mahatma Gandhi's World...*, 194.

159 Mathai, *Mahatma Gandhi's World...*, 196.

160 Mathai, *Mahatma Gandhi's World...*, 197.

nourish and compliment the early century Christian schema. The derived convergence serves to be a new paradigm for Indian context.

Evaluation

Dwight Hopkins an eminent African American theologian comments, "To be a Christian

in any time period is to practice a preferential option for the poor."[161] The concerns of wealth and poverty, its legitimate purpose, catalyzed by recent economic recessions have all raised alarms for constructing a "just" and "enough" economic model. The Church in India has an issue at hand, to be dealt in detail drawing inspiration from the Patristic model as well as the Indian milieu.

As Amartya Sen comments on the India's slow progress in removing social and economic inequality, suggests that "this progress can be made more effective through committed public action and participatory activities" (*The Argumentative Indian*) .What is required is an integrated approach to development and growth. Growth is not independent of the social transformation (of an economy).[162] And the converging paradigm of Clement and Gandhi indeed provides a revitalized transformative approach for Indian situation.

Conclusion

In the Introduction to Indian Philosophy S. Radhakrishnan pens it succinctly, "the Indian never felt that the world was a field of battle where men struggled for power, wealth and domination.[163] For India concern for poor and *oikos* comes naturally, the Divine is sought even in the vegetation, the earth is referred to as Mother, and Greed is contemplated as sin and fellowship with ecology celebrated. However, the irony remains that these ideas are seldom recalled while we run towards exploiting the resources of nature and are overcome by greed at various levels. Ever increasing poverty issues, malnourished

161 Joerg Rieger, ed., *Opting for the Margins: Postmodernity and Liberation in Christian Theology* (New York: Oxford University Press, 2003), 19.

162 http://www.livemint.com/Politics/hqZ776khE3VfUp9gbIdyML/Growth-alone-not-enough-to-fight-poverty-Amartya-Sen.html (12/08/2015).

163 S. Radhakrishnan, *Indian Philosophy*, Vol. I (New Delhi: Oxford, 1999), 22.

population and exploitation of ecology are all to be dealt in single thread. An unbroken wholeness, a personal piety, a Divine attitude is demanded as Paulos Mar Gregorios has repeatedly pressed upon, "the interrelatedness of God-Man-Universe and respectful approach to created order."

Autarchy in Clement of Alexandria indeed provides a lead into this profound thought process, to move empathetically ahead into the future with an individual as well as a corporate idea of Greed line. An anthropological boundary of the boundless Providence.

Chapter 4

Conclusion

In a context of globalized economy and social structures, sensitivity and concern towards the poor and marginalized are often unattended. The cries for Socio-economic justice is often suppressed and isolated by the Globalized capitalist forces. Atrocities against the marginalized and poor in society are scaling high in swift pace, social and economic marginalization of voices is on the rise. Governmental policies and its implementation are often found capsized by corrupt forces in the economy. International agencies and social committed organizations either seize to raise voice or are often forgotten in policy making. Also, in the relevant context of Indian socio-economic problems and issues such as wide spread caste discrimination, poverty, income disparity, corruption, etc. there is a need for strong social commitment and action. Human beings are discriminated, exposed and exploited on basis of class, creed, income and gender. Social sensitivity and Justice remains numb to the concerns of the weak. Christian communities and individuals should evolve means of eradicating these issues, drawing potential from the Redemptive liberation and Salvation offered by Christ for humankind.

Christianity is a religion based on an historical revelation and therefore by its very nature is involved in the world in which it lives. From its very beginnings the authors of the New Testament have already reflected on the relation between the message of salvation which Christ proclaimed and the social and political environments surrounding the new religion.[164] Their thoughts are still being adopted, developed and adapted to new historical circumstances. Social sensitivity and concern for the poor remains the very important facet of Christian Philanthropic efforts. Interestingly to note, Friedrich Schleiermacher expounds a theme of and God-consciousness merging to become one in self consciousness. As Schleiermacher who was convinced that delving into the mystery of the divine being apart from the world violated the nature of theology itself. In the closing pages of the *The Christian faith*, Schleiermacher declared,

We have only to do with the God-consciousness given in our self-consciousness along with our consciousness of the world; hence we have no formula for the being of God in Himself as distinct from the being of God in the world, and should have to borrow any such formula from speculation, and so prove ourselves disloyal to the character of the discipline at which we are working.[165]

The ethical models of Justice, sufficiency, enough, contentment are all vital for contemporary global context. In the backdrop of Ecological, Social and Economical concerns a *sufficiency* or *enough* models are much sought after. World Council of Churches envisages a culture of 'enough,' of sharing and caring and the concept of *Autarchy* (self sufficiency) as in Clement of Alexandria prove to be a genuine urge for "enough", "contentment" on an individual as well as a corporate level. The Culture of Self-sufficiency is of varied facets and functions, It can be an upper limit for consumerist attitudes, It can also serve as an internal factor to generate a feeling of *satisfaction, contentment*, or *enough* in the globalized era of markets determining our consumptions (an unhindered drive to grow by exploiting).

In India the thrust on poverty eradication is visible in governmental policies since independence; however, this inevitable and crucial project remains unattained up to large extent for a developing nation like Indian, in a wider global situation. As per *The*

164 Peter C. Phan, *Social Thought* (U.S.A: Michael Glazier, Inc, 1984), 13.

165 Stanley J. Grenz, *The Social God and the Relational Self* (London: Westminster John Knox Press, 2001), 25.

Millennium Development Goals Report 2015, "Nearly 60 per cent of the world's 1 billion extremely poor people lived in just five countries in 2011: India, Nigeria, China, Bangladesh and the Democratic Republic of the Congo (ranked from high to low)."[166] And it is more alarming as the report says that women face a greater risk of living in poverty.

Christianity is always a religion in transition. It progresses, develops, renews and reinvents itself as part of the constantly changing world.[167] The contemporary engagements with culture, religions, ethnicity, traditions have all to be assimilated in Theologizing. Contextual theology succinctly defined is a way of doing theology in which one has to take into account the *Kerygma* and the contemporary context; the tradition of the Christian people; the culture in which one is theologizing, and the social change in that culture. Clement clearly qualifies in these aspects as a contextual theologian of his times.

Clement also has a very contemporary relevance in context of religious pluralism. He is away from any exclusivist claims or hegemony in pluralistic context. As Norman Russell comments, "Clement may castigate some of the religious practices of his non-Christian contemporaries, but he does not feel threatened by them. His Euhemerism[168] gave him an overall unifying theory which enabled him to see all manifestations of polytheism in rationalist terms as the fruit of human deification."[169]

Clement of Alexandria is a prominent figure from the patristic period in whom theologians today find a precedent for positive interaction with other religions. They point out to some illustrative, examples from Clement, such as, that in his Exhortation to the heathen:

---

166 *The Millenium Development Goals Report* (United Nations Secretariat), Department of Economic and Social Affairs, United Nations, 2015.

167 Angie Pears, *Doing Contextual Theology* (New York: Routledge, 2010), 1.

168 Euhemerism is the interpretation of myths as traditional accounts of historical persons and events.

169 Russell, Norman, *The Doctrine of Deification in the Greek Patristic Tradition* (New York: Oxford University Press, 2004), 125.

"...the Greeks, having received certain scintillations of the divine word, have given forth some utterances of truth, they bear indeed witness that the force of truth is not hidden..."

Clement also suggests that God gave philosophy to the Greeks as a kind of scripture, leading them to the fullness of the truth, which they will find in the Logos. This can be seen for example, in *Stromata* 1.5:

Perchance, too, philosophy was given to the Greeks directly and primarily, till the Lord should call the Greeks. For this was a schoolmaster to bring "the Hellenic mind," as the law, the Hebrews, "to Christ". Philosophy, therefore, was a preparation, paving the way for him who is perfected in Christ.[170]

Furthermore, *In Orthodox Christians and Islam in Postmodern Age*, Metropolitan George Khodr [171] writes ..."In thought of Clement of Alexandria, the divine Word speaks to the entire world, and God justifies mankind through numerous salvation paths. God is not only the God of Isreal, he is also the Saviour of the World, and appears to be engaged throughout the world by means of multiple faces of his wisdom."

Clement of Alexandria stands out as one of the earliest systematic Christian thinker, who provides the latter years of Christian thought a contextual theological premise to operate and flourish. Ethics, Moral Philosophy and Hermeneutics are often much sought after categories in Clement. The enormous treasure of Greek philosophical thought is synthesized by Clement for the furtherance of Christian Theology. As David Runia remarks, Clement is 'constantly in dialogue with his source', giving his material a new thrust in accordance with his Christian convictions.[172]

Autarchy in Clement of Alexandria catalyzes an inner detachment or self-sufficiency mode in life. This self-sufficiency is not self acclaimed, rather it is a gracious gift in union with

---

170 Andrew M. Sharp, *Orthodox Christians and Islam in Postmodern Age* (The Netherlands: Brill Publications, 2012), 60.

171 Most Reverend Metropolitan George (Khodr) of the Byblos and Botris (Mount Lebanon) is the metropolitan of the archdiocese of Byblos and Botris (Mount Lebanon) of the Church of Antioch.

172 Norman Russell, 124.

the providence of God. Autarchy calls forth a refined attitude to wealth, material goods, to self itself. Autarchy as a condition transforms the self itself, hence the prefix of self in self-sufficiency itself is transformed. Autarchy in Clement traverses from Platonic, Aristotelian, or Stoic ideal to a virtues reward in communion with and in God. Autarchy is not the product of human efforts but grace received in communion with God. *Theosis* is the zenith of human efforts, and autarchy the en-route privilege enjoyed by an individual who enters this journeying towards *Theosis*.

The existing global culture is often plagued by the passion to consume and possess. The unreasoned boast abounds that the good life is found in accumulation idea that "more is better". Indeed we often accept this notion without question, with the result that the lust for affluence in contemporary society has become psychotic: it has completely lost touch with reality. Furthermore, the pace of the modern world accentuates our sense of being fractured and fragmented. We feel strained, hurried, and breathless. The complexity of rushing to achieve and accumulate more and more frequently threatens to overwhelm us; it seems there is no escape from the rat race. Rephrasing and in the same vein as, Richard J. Foster opines of simplicity in Christian life, *Autarkia* frees us from this modern obsession. It ushers judgment to our obsessive profligacy, and calms our frantic and consumerist attitudes. It liberates from us from what William Penn called "cumber". It allows us to see material things for what they are-goods to enhance life. People once again become more important than possessions. It enables us to live lives of integrity in the face of the terrible realities of our global village.[173]

It is pivotal to stress that in a context of grave socio-economic and ecological concerns for sustainability, poverty alleviation, and reducing income disparity, a model of *Autarkia* is quintessential. Simplicity, moral and ethical contentment are all sought after virtues in Indian philosophical traditions.

The Self as even in this research *Self sufficiency (Autarchy)* is a subject of great significance in theological parlance. Defining the self has been a critical subject in every field of study. The far

173 Foster, Richard J. *Freedom of Simplicity* (New York: Harper & Row Publishers, 1981), 3.

spread discussions on the categories of self and the other needs some thought. Interestingly as Oliver Davies explicates, "In the modern world our encounter with otherness, with the alien or strange, begins not at the borders of the self, but rather within the self, at the very core of our identity, and in a way that challenges the self-possession of the subject..."[174]

In Levinasian[175] and Derridean[176] thought the autonomous *cogito* of the self at the centre of philosophical thought is replaced by the Other. One can easily trace a shift in the Post modern understanding of self from that of Cartesian self. The deconstructed self appears to be a non-self,[177] rather a self which is understood in relation to the other. The post modern emphasis on the dissolution of the self can and sometimes does–claim a venerable religious heritage. One can cite the *anatta* doctrine of Theravada Buddhism, the assaults on self carried out in Zen Buddhism, or the tradition of the *via negativa* within the Christian tradition.[178]

Autarkia seeks communion, a social character and as John D. Zizuolas opines "Communion seems to strike a sensitive chord in a Christian world fed up with individualism and institutional rigidity."[179] Self sufficiency extends a responsibility towards others, a social character of selfhood,[180] 'a social solidarity', as Niebuhr notes in 'The Responsible Self'[181]

Thus, Self as in Self sufficiency is not a narrowed, egoistic, individual self but develops into a wider understanding encompassing

174 Andrew Shepherd, *The Gift of the Other* (Cambridge: James Clarke & Co., 2014), 100.

175 Thought of Emmanuel Levinas, the French Philosopher.

176 Thought of Jacques Derridda, the French Philosopher.

177 Shepherd, *The Gift of the Other* ..., 99.

178 Edith Wyschogrod, David Crownfield and Carl A. Raschke, eds., *Lacan and Theological Discourse* (New York: State University of New York Press, 1989), 19.

179 John D. Zizioulas, *Communion and Otherness* (London: T & T Clark, 2006), 14.

180 H. Richard Niebuhr, *The Responsible Self* (San Francisco: Harper and Row Publishers, 1978), 71.

181 Niebuhr, *The Responsible Self*..., 65.

the other. The other is vital for the self; or rather the other defines the self. The self sufficiency is also primarily the sufficiency of others and develops in communion. Autarchy is not just the self sufficiency of one's self but an escalation towards the contentment of society with Divine providence. *Autarchy* in Clement of Alexandria as an ethical and moral concept instigates towards a new paradigm for constructing *Greed line* in Indian context; a paradigm for sufficiency, enough and legitimate consumption.

Appendix 1

The Ascent of Humanity: A Trajectory for Theological Anthropology in Context of Global Refugee & Migration Crisis

Anthropology claims to be an inclusive discipline, with *anthropos*, "human kind," as its object of study. The natural sciences, philosophy, history, theology, classical studies, and even jurisprudence have all been called upon in order to throw light on this exploration of human beings in all their complexity.[182] Anthropology is indeed a subject great relevance and of contemporary importance for Theology in this century. Theology cannot just be a talk about God; rather it has to deal with human person in relation to the Divine. The categories of God, essence (*ousia*), person, Christology has all relational aspect to the human person. The anthropological stance of Christian Theology has to be widened and profoundly discussed to envisage a better understanding of humanity. The Divine image (*imagio dei*), the perpetual essence of divinity and scars of sin all need vital treatment in Theological anthropology.

182 Fiona Bowie. *The Anthropology of Religion* (U.S.A: Blackwell Publishing, 2006), 1.

The object of Theology itself has been understood at times as study of human beings rather than metaphysical speculation concerning the nature of God by people like Ludwig Feuerbach (1804-72).[183] Emil Brunner argues, humanity must first of all be defined theologically; only then may the philosopher, the psychologists and the biologist make their statements. This insistence flows from the conviction that, in the final analysis, human beings cannot be understood in terms of themselves. Rather, our identity must be anchored in something greater or transcendent-ultimately God our creator. Interestingly the word 'identity' comes from the Latin word *idem*, which means "same". This identity exploration leads to relationalities which are embedded in the core meaning.[184] In his classic work The Nature and Destiny of Man, American theologian Reinhold Niebuhr observed that humanity is a puzzling paradox- the paradox of our place in the cosmos.[185] Humanity as the centre of the cosmos on one hand and otherwise dazzled by our place in the larger canvas of the cosmos. Hence, it is relational on twin spheres, to self and the other. As Orthodox Theologian Stavros Yangazoglou enumerates it, "the human is not to be defined statically. Man is not merely biological or spiritual existence, but a beginning in relation and en route. The fullness of existence is not itself- referentiality but the encounter and communion with absolute Other, with an existence radically beyond and outside his own."[186]

However, it is disappointing to note that much of corresponding early Christian wealth of Theological Anthropology, Socio-economic sensitivity and the Philosophical tradition of Patristics remain unexplored in contemporary discussions. Christian Church possesses in its literature an abundant and incomparable treasure. But it is

---

183 Fiona Bowie. *The Anthropology of Religion* (U.S.A: Blackwell Publishing, 2006), 2.

184 Richard J. Plantinga, Thomas R. Thompson and Mathew D. Lundberg. *An Introduction to Christian Theology* (Cambridge: Cambridge University Press, 2010), 181.

185 Richard J. Plantinga, Thomas R. Thompson and Mathew D. Lundberg. *An Introduction to Christian Theology* (Cambridge: Cambridge University Press, 2010), 180.

186 http://www.ocms.ac.uk/regnum/downloads/Orthodox_Handbook_on_Ecumenism-Watermarked.pdf (6/04/2016).

an inheritance that must be reclaimed by each generation.[187] Also, Anthropological understanding in the larger context of growing global atrocities on humanity wielded by humanity itself, the issues of immigrants and refugees from war torn nations are all relevant.

St. Clement of Alexandria explains that man is the "most important work" of creation and the only one whose soul was endowed with intelligence and wisdom and whose body was adorned with beauty and harmony. Man is the only being who has been aware of the existence of God ever since he was created.[188] However, all these splendours are nothing but consequences of God's image, after which man was created. Also, *Theosis* or Deification was a very pivotal concept for Clement of Alexandria. Clement made claims of humankind's eventual deification that were anything but subtle. "I say, the Word of God became a man, so that you might learn from a man how to become a god" and "men are gods and men" or more interestingly an Indian Advaitic parallel can be seen in Clement when he writes, It is then, as appears, the greatest of all lessons to know one's self. For if one knows himself, he will know God; and knowing God, he will be made like God, not by wearing gold or long robes, but by well-doing, and by requiring as few things as possible (*The Instructor*, Book III, Chapter I).

Moreover, Clement of Alexandria did not maintain the doctrine of the pre-existence of human souls as many of his contemporaries did. According to him, the souls were created together with the body and at the beginning were not equal to angels. However, in his opinion, there is not an inseparable gap between human souls and angels; souls are immortal and through spiritual progress the souls of perfect gnostics can attain equality to angels even here in this life and, finally, after death (Clement's concept of *isangelia*).[189] As St. Gregory the Great puts it, Man is "animal being made God". In the perspective of the dialectical relationship between created an

187 Henry Chadwick. ed., *Alexandrian Christianity* (Great Britain: Westminster Press, 1954), 9.

188 http://orthodox-theology.com/media/PDF/IJOT3-2011/Stan-Human.pdf (8/04/2016).

189 Matyas Havrda, Vit Husek and Jana Platova eds., *The Seventh Book of the Stromateis* (Netherlands: Brill Publications, 2012), 97.

uncreated, as manifested in patristic Christology. Male and female, body-soul, the whole man is the image of God. He is not immortal, neither in the body nor in soul, he is immortal in the perspective of the life in Christ, when he is open to communion with other and with the eminent Other. If now in history the ontology of the human person in Christ is iconic, "in a mirror dimly" (Cor 13:12), to the escaton of the kingdom will the fullness of the "likeness of God" shall be revealed. For Gregory of Nyssa all of humanity is created in the image of God and indeed to display this image is what it means to be truly human. This quality is a part of human nature and common to all people:

"It is indeed within your reach; you have within yourselves the standard by which to apprehend the Divine. For He who made you did at the same time endow your nature with this wonderful quality. For God imprinted on it the likeness of the glories of His own Nature, as if moulding the form of a carving into wax."[190] Also, while Clement accepted the Platonist view that the soul is independent of the body, he rejected the Gnostic teaching that the soul was sent into this world as punishment. Like St. Justin he held that the soul is not immortal by nature, but as a gift in Christ.[191]

Humanity is certainly the focal point of all pertaining discussions and issues of contemporary relevance. The immigrants and refugee crisis (Syrian), ecological concerns, Bioethics, Socio-economic concerns all seem essentially calling for a better understanding of Humanity. It is not a thought as in Modernity of 'Man at the centre'; rather it is the post modern idea of 'Man in relation to the other' as well as the Divine which ought to be explored. The patristic thought as in Clement and others provides profound insights into this thought process and embellishes Anthropological understanding. The Divine Image of God in you and me seeks for an affirmation of Humanity on the basis of Theology, Justice, Love and Compassion. 'You are gods' as for Clement and 'Tat tvam asi' ('You are that', *Chandogya*

190 Johannes Quasten, and Joseph Plumpe ed., *Gregory of Nyssa, The Lord's Prayer, the Beatitudes, vol. 18, Ancient Christian Writers* (New York: Paulist Press, 1954), 148.

191 http://www.orthodoxytoday.org/view/de-beer-genesis-creation-and-evolution (7/07/2016).

Upanishads) as in Indian Thought. Lets realize the Divine in each other and of that yearning towards the The Divine, being gratified by considering the displaced, the homeless and migrants.

Namasthe ! I bow to the Divine in you..

Fr. Anish John

Appendix 2

Linking Poverty, Wealth and Ecology: A Convergence of Basilian* and Gandhian Socio-Economic Thought

(The title of this paper owes its debt to the WCC published work to advance economic, social and ecological justice since the 9th Assembly in Porto Alegre till the 10th WCC Assembly at Busan. The consultations on poverty, wealth and ecology organized by WCC Poverty, Wealth and Ecology (PWE) project are also catalyst for this work)

Introduction

The insights offered by the prolific Fathers of the Patristic age continue to reverberate with striking and contemporary relevance,[192] but remains scanty in most of the contemporary discussions. Insights

192* St. Basil, the Great. The province of Cappadocia (Asia Minor) just before the middle of fourth century produced three great theologians, Basil of Caesarea, his friend Gregory of Nazianzus and his brother Gregory of Nyssa whom we refer to as "the Cappadocian Fathers". Among the three Cappadocians, St. Basil (330-379 C.E) earned the title of the 'Great' on account of his outstanding qualifications as an ecclesiastical statesman and organizer, as a great exponent of Christian doctrine, as the Father of oriental monasticism, as reformer of liturgy, and as an effective social activist.
Susan R. Holman ed., *Wealth and Poverty in Early Church and Society* (U.S.A.: Baker Academic, 2008), 7.

in the areas of wealth, poverty and Social Justice are found ample in St. Basil, the Great (4th Century). He offers an articulated theology, sensitive to social concerns as in the modern liberation and subaltern perspectives.. The widening wealth disparities, poverty, preferential option for poor, Justice, overcoming Greed, economy of Life, etc., are all implications for theological discussion in Indian context with special emphasis on Gandhian thought.

St. Basil shares with St. John Chrysostom the notion that those who possess great resources but refuse to help others are guilty of a kind of theft. It is important to note that Basil is interested not only in ameliorating the plight of the poor, but also in identifying and reforming the structures that create and reinforce the cycle of poverty.[193] Let us briefly identify and evaluate his socio-economic concerns.

Criticism of Luxury or Extravaganza

St. Basil staunchly criticized the wealthy for their excessive consumption and the luxurious life style in his days. There were different forms of extravaganzas unleashed by the rich in society, the accumulation of wealth, resources, pompous show of infrastructures in form of houses adorned with luxuries, horse–carriages, servants for various needs, and lavish burials, etc., were just some of these. He writes in his homily *To the Rich*, "some wealth for spending, and some held in reserve, while the allowance for daily provisions should exceed the level of mere necessities. Some will be for comforts within the house, and some outward display; some to make travelling comfortable, and some to make life splendid and luxuries at home. I am overwhelmed even at the thought of so many contrived extravagances!"

The irony of the times as observed by St. Basil was the striking contrast between haves and have- not, as observed in developing economies of this cent. He writes, "You gorgeously array your walls, but do not clothe your fellow human being; you adorn horses, but

193 Paul C. Schroeder, *On Social Justice* (New York: SVS Press, 2009), 29-30.

turn away from the shameful plight of your brother or sister; you allow grain to rot in your barns, but ignore the oppressed!"[194]

Wealth is required to keep up with the bare necessities in life; Basil enumerates the use of wealth in following passage, "after all, what is the use of wealth?" Do you wish to wrap yourself in fine apparel? Surely two lengths of cloth are sufficient for a coat, while the covering of a single garment fulfills every need with regard to clothing. Or would you spend your wealth on food? A loaf of bread is enough to fill your stomach. Why then do you grieve? Of what have you been deprived?[195]

Rejection of Usury

St. Basil talks about usury as inhumanity and injustice towards fellow human beings, unleashed by the rich in society in his homily *Against lending with interest* (on Psalm XV). He vividly critics the rich for lending money to the poor at high interest and condemns it as sin; Rather one should give without expecting anything in return, "Lend to those from whom there is no hope of repayment" (Lk 6:34).

Basil begins developing his arguments by quoting the Old Testament, prophets Ezekiel and Jeremiah, who spoke against the prevailing practice of usury in society,

> "...the prophet, describing the perfect man who has suffered through life, recounted, among the many exploits worthy of a man, the fact that he had never lent his money for interest. In many passages of the scripture, lending with interest is condemned as sinful. Thus, Ezekiel places taking interest among the major evils (Ezek 22:12) and the Law clearly forbids it: "you shall not demand interest from your brother and your neighbor" (Deut 23:20). Elsewhere it is said: Deceit upon deceit, usury upon usury" (Jer 9:5). And of the city that prospers on a multitude of sins, it is said in the psalm: "Usury and fraud never depart from its streets" (Ps 55:12). And the prophet, pointing out something as the mark or seal of human perfection, says: "He never lent

194 Ibid., 26.

195 Ibid., 44.

> his money for interest." Indeed, it is extremely inhuman that one has to beg for the most basic necessities to support his life while another is not satisfied with the capital he has, but excogitates ways of increasing his opulence at the expense of the poor in distress."[196]

Sharing and lending without expecting a return is held as of high value, give to the poor and God will bless you through the poor. "Rich men, listen to the advice that, in view of your inhumanity, we give to the poor: Bear any suffering rather than the calamities that will come from usury. But if you obey the Lord, you will not need such an advice. Now, what does the Lord advice? "Lend to those from whom there is no hope of repayment" (Lk 6:34). But, you say, how can it be called "lending" if there is no hope of repayment? Try to understand the meaning of the Lord's saying and you will admire the goodness of that Law. When you give to the poor for the love of God, the same thing is both gift and loan. Gift, first, because there is no hope of receiving anything in return; loan, secondly, because the Lord will reward you abundantly through the poor and because for such a trifle that you give to them, you will receive huge sums in return."[197]

Receiving interest from the poor is the worst crime against humanity. Basil puts it as "If you take from the poor, you commit the worse crime of inhumanity: you derive profit from miseries, you gain money from tears, you oppress the needy, and you starve the hungry. You have no mercy whatever; you do not realize the bond you have with those who suffer. And yet you call acts of humanity the profits you receive. "Woe to those who call evil good, and good evil, who change darkness into light and light into darkness and change bitter into sweet, and sweet into bitter" (Isa 5:20) and those who give the name of philanthropy to the hatred of man."[198]

196 Peter C. Phan, *Social Thought* (U.S.A: Michael Glazier, 1984), 111.

197 Ibid., 112.

198 Johannes Quasten, *Patrology* (U.S.A: Christian Classics, 1996), 112.

Sharing the Wealth with the Poor- *koinos*

Throughout the Basil's homilies on social themes, one of the most commonly repeated words is the Greek adjective *Koinos,* meaning "shared" or "common", a cognate of the word *Koinonia* or "communion". Basil uses this word repeatedly to underscore what is for him a basic moral premise: the world was created for the common benefit of all, and given by God to humanity for their shared use.

He especially delights in using nature images to illustrate this point; For example, in his homily *In the Time of Famine and Drought,* Basil says,

> "The animals use in common the plants that grow naturally from the earth. Flocks of sheep graze together upon one and the same hillside, herds of horses feed upon the same plain, and all living creatures permit each other to satisfy their need for food. But we hoard what is common, and keep for ourselves what belongs to many others."[199]

St. Basil highlights the importance of sharing wealth with the poor, the wealth left unshared and piled up gets unproductive:

"Like a mighty river that is divided into many streams in order to irrigate the fertile soil, so also are those who give their wealth to be divided up and distributed in the houses of the poverty-stricken. Wells become more productive if they are drained completely, while they silt up if they left standing. Thus wealth left idle is of no use to anyone, but put to use and exchanged it becomes fruitful and beneficial for the public..." (*I will tear down my Barns*).

"Give to the man who begs from you; do not turn your back on the man who borrows from you" (Mt 5:42). This saying of our Lord invites us to adopt the spirit of sharing, mutual love and what is proper to our nature. Man, indeed, is a political and social animal. Now, in social relations and in common life, a certain disposition to share one's goods is necessary in order to assist the needy. "Give to those who beg from you." Our Lord asks that for charity's sake we should be ready to give to those who ask; moreover, for the sake of reason, we should discern the needs of each one who asks.

199 Paul C. Schroeder, op.cit., 31.

From the Acts of the Apostles we learn how this was carried out by those who accomplish wisely the purposes of religion. "nor was there anyone needy among them, for all who owned property or houses sold them and donated the proceeds; they used to lay them at the feet of the Apostles to be distributed to everyone according to his need". (Acts 4:34-35).[200]

Lack of sharing is compared to murder by St. Basil in his Homily delivered in times of famine and drought. "The pain of starvation, from which the hungry die, is a horrible suffering. Of all human calamities, famine is the principle one, and the most miserable of death is, no doubt that by starvation... now what punishment should not be inflicted upon the one who passes by such a body? What cruelty can surpass that? How can we not count him as a sacrilegious person and a murderer? The person, who can cure such an infirmity and because of avarice refuses his medicine, can with reason be condemned as a murderer."[201]

Injustice and Impact on Nature

St. Basil speaks of how the earth itself does not discriminate between rich and poor or between owners and non-owners. The nature provides us with fruits and crops to sustain everyone's need but the greedy exploit it for own greed.

"The earth was welcoming all to its richness: it germinated the crops deep in the furrows, produced large clusters of grapes on the vine, made the olive tree bend under a vast quantity of fruit, and offered every delicious variety of the fruit tree. But the rich man was unwelcoming and unfruitful; he did not even possess as yet, and already he begrudged the needy." As may be noted from these passages, basil regards the selfishness of human behavior as a kind of anomaly within creation. Although, competition within and among species is a normal part of the natural order, only humans compete in such way as to take more than they actually need or can possibly use, while depriving others of what is necessary for their survival. Throughout the homilies, Basil describes the phenomenon of human

200 Peter C. Phan, op.cit., 110.

201 Peter C. Phan, op.cit., 119.

overconsumption through the categories of disease, compulsion, and addiction. At one point, basil says such selfish behaviors can only be attributed to "some device concocted by the devil," since no rational foundation or basis in actual need can be found for them.[202]

Basil is of the opinion that the rich man who does not share his possessions with others commits injustice, which in turn causes natural disasters; He explains social injustices as a cause for natural disaster and says...

"We know that the Lord sends us all these plagues because we have separated ourselves from him and because we have been negligent in his service, not in order to exterminate us but to correct us. The Lord acts like our good parents, concerned about the welfare of their children; they become angry against their children and punish them, not because they desire to do them harm, but because they want to correct their youthful carelessness and to draw them away from their sinful ways and back to the path of virtue..."

What then, is the cause of such disorder and confusion? What is the reason for the new things, in these days? Let us investigate this, since we are rational beings. Is it because there is no one to govern the universe? Is it because God, the best of artists, has neglected his administration? Is it because he has lost all power and authority?..

No, the reason why we are not governed in the usual way is clear and self-evident: we receive, but give to nobody; we praise charity, but do not practice it to the needy. Slaves we were, and we have been made free, and yet we do not have sympathy for those who are needy. We have God as our unfailing provider and dispenser, and yet we have shown ourselves niggardly and close-fisted towards the poor. Our ewes have produced numerous sucklings, and yet the poor are more numerous than our ewes. Our barns and granaries are too tight for what we store in them, and yet we ourselves do not have compassion for those who suffer from tight circumstances. For all these things we are threatened with a just sentence. If God does not open his hands for us, it is because we have cast out brotherly love..."[203]

---

202 Paul C. Schroeder, *On Social Justice* (New York: SVS Press, 2009), 31-32.

203 Peter C. Phan, op.cit., 118-119.

Use of Wealth and Eschatology

Christ teaches his disciples through the parable of *Unjust Steward* to 'make friends by unrighteous mammon, that when you fail, they may receive you into an everlasting home' (Lk 16:9).The steward is unjust in his actions, which are not condoned, but his shrewdness is praised.[204]

Basil regards wealth as a means to build up treasure in heaven, if you want storehouses; you have them in the stomachs of the poor. By sharing what is temporal you will be invited to share in what is eternal. Lay up for yourself treasure in heaven. The things there are not devoured by moths, nor are they spoiled by corruption, nor do thieves break in and steal them. Oh how desirable these words will appear to you on the day of judgment: "come, you that are blessed by my father, inherit the kingdom prepared for you from the foundation of the world; for I was hungry and you gave me no food, I was thirsty and you gave me nothing to drink, I was naked and you did not give me, clothing."[205]

Basil reminds not to neglect the opportune moment, nor pass over the present time, waiting for some other chance, lest we should be lost in the end on account of our hesitation and delaying. 'Consider carefully, I ask you, both the present and the future; do not betray the latter from a shameful motive of profit. The body, your outward manifestation in this life, will forsake you in the end at the appearance of the expected Judge- and come He most certainly will- you will shut yourself out of the distribution of heavenly glory and honor. Instead of the enduring and blessed life, you will enter into the unquenchable fire of hell and bitter ages of agony. Basil testifies that the last judgment and second coming are not fanciful tales or 'imaginary stories' to frighten, rather 'reality foretold by the voice of truth'.

The body that has disintegrated in the grave will arise and will be reunited with the very same soul from which it was separated by death. Then a careful examination of each person's life will take

204 Joseph Allen, Gen.ed., *The Orthodox Study Bible* (U.S.A: Thomas Nelson Publishers, 1997), 181.

205 Mt 25:34-36

place, in which no others will testify, but rather one's own conscience will bear witness. Everyone will then receive due reward from the just Judge.[206]

Basil narrates the second coming and judgment on the social insensitivity by quoting the Scripture "...to whom the king says when he appears come you that are blessed by my father, inherit the kingdom prepared for you from the foundation of the world; for I was hungry and you gave me food, I was thirsty and you gave me something to drink, I was a stranger and you welcomed me, I was naked and you gave me clothing, I was sick and in prison, and you came to me."[207]

The New City: *Basiliad*

The New City or *Basiliad* was an ideal city, a self equipped shelter for the common man in society. A city idealized by social commitments and provisions for the marginalized. In Gregory of Nazianzus' funeral oration for Basil, Gregory describes the practical legacy of Basil's philanthropic endeavors in this way: "go forth a little way from the city, and behold the new city, the storehouse of piety, the common treasury of the wealthy ...where disease is regarded in a religious light, and disaster is thought a blessing, and sympathy is put to the test." Gregory is referring to the great philanthropic foundation founded by Basil that later came to be known as the Basiliad. Here the poor and diseased were able to receive food, shelter, and medical treatment free of charge.[208] Basiliad in its early institution seems to have had its roots in Basil's philanthropic efforts to provide assistance to victims of the drought and famine in 369 (C.E). During the famine basil sold and distributed his parental inheritance, to help the starving populace of Caesarea.

Basiliad expanded significantly during basil's Episcopal ministry, partly through the patronage of Emperor Valens and the support of other benefactors. It eventually grew into a large complex of buildings that not only served as a distribution center for donated

206 Paul C. Schroeder, *On Social Justice* (New York: SVS Press, 2009), 88.

207 Mt 25:34-36

208 Paul C. Schroeder, op.cit., 33.

goods, but also provided shelter to the homeless and skilled medical services to the sick, especially treatment for leprosy with its associated social stigma. Basil himself was known for his willingness to care for the victims of leprosy personally, thus providing an example for others to follow, as Gregory recounts in his funeral oration:

"He did not therefore disdain to honor with his lips this disease, noble and of noble ancestry and brilliant reputation though he was, but saluted them as brethren...Basil's care was for the sick, and the relief of their wounds, and the imitation of Christ, by cleansing leprosy, not by a word, but in deed."[209] The new town contained institutions such as some kind of hospital; residences for travelers and the poor; residences for clergy; the bishop's palace; a leper hospital; and small factories or workshops for teaching and practicing trades.[210]

The Indian Context

For India enormous social sensitivity and philanthropic fervor is knit in its socio-cultural fabric. Remarkably, the moral, ethical and Socio-economic view in Gandhian thought is a significant milieu for Indian context. However, the Indian context of far-flung economic disparities, poverty issues raises alarms to a social sensitivity and ethical concern. One in three of the world's poorest people are living in India, the world's second-fastest growing economy, according to a new study by the World Bank.[211]

About 30 crore people still live in extreme poverty in India even as the Millennium Development Goal (MGD) programme will expire in December, as per reports of United Nations. India, adopted the United Nation's MGD in 2000 with an aim to free millions from extreme poverty, hunger, illiteracy and poor health.[212]

---

209 Ibid., 35.

210 Susan R. Holman ed., *Wealth and Poverty in Early Church and Society* (U.S.A: Baker Academic, 2008), 269.

211 http://www.telegraph.co.uk/news/worldnews/asia/india/10003228/India-has-one-third-of-worlds-poorest-says-World-Bank.html (12/08/2015).

212 http://timesofindia.indiatimes.com/india/30-crore-people-still-live-in-extreme-poverty-in-India-UN-report/articleshow/46122767.cms (12/08/2015).

Gandhian Thought

Gandhian socio-economic thought serves as a platter for analyzing Indian context. The widespread economic and social disparities condole as perils of unprecedented Globalization. Gandhian thought offers a wide set of alternatives to the crisis global economies face today; *Sarvodaya*, *Ramarajya* (kingdom of love, Justice and Righteousness), *Asteya* (Non-stealing), *Aparigraha* (Renunciation), *Ahimsa* (Non-injury) are some pivotal features. The Gandhian frame of reference is largely inherited from the Upanishadic- Gita tradition and notion of *Atman* as its centre.[213] Furthermore, the Gandhian economic philosophy like his political, social and religious philosophy is based on *Satyagraha*[214] and *Ahimsa*.[215, 216] Albert Schweitzer and several other Christian interpreters of Gandhian thought consider the emphasis on social service to be indicative of Christian influence on Gandhi.[217]

Selected Gandhian Economic and Ethical Features

Non-stealing

According to Gandhi it is theft (1) to take anything belonging to another without his permission, even if it be with his knowledge; (2) to take something in the belief that it is nobody's property, for e.g., things found on the roadside; (3) to take something from another even with his permission if we have no real need of it; (4) to improperly multiply our wants; (5) to desire acquisition of anything belonging to others.[218] What is most significant and what lends an added contemporary relevance to Gandhi's exegesis of the age-old ethical principle of non-stealing is that he related it to life-styles and the consequent grinding poverty affecting millions of people all

---

213 V.T. Patil. e.d., *Studies on Gandhi* (New Delhi: Sterling Publishers, 1983), 5.

214 Insistence on Truth.

215 Non-violence, Love.

216 J.S. Mathur. e.d., *Gandhian Thought and Contemporary Society* (Bombay: Bhartiya Vidya Bhavan, 1974), 255.

217 T.S. Devadoss, *Sarvodaya* (Madras: University of Madras, 1974), 83.

218 M.P. Mathai, *Mahatma Gandhi's World-View* (New Delhi: Gandhi Peace Foundation, 2000), 131.

over the world. One is reminded of Emile Zola's deeply disturbing comment: "behind every great fortune is a crime."[219]

Non-Possession

As Prof. M.P. Mathai remarks (*Mahatma Gandhi's World-View*), "For Gandhi, possession of superfluous things was a crime against God and Humanity. If each retained possession only of what he needed, no one could be in want, and all would be in contentment." In the contemporary world-experience of resource depletion, drying up of sources of energy and other related ecological problems the vow of non-possession, though seemingly impossible and subjective must be kept constantly in view and in its light our possession must be critically re-examined and reduced progressively and voluntarily.[220]

Yajna or Sacrifice

According to Gandhi, "*Yajna* means an act directed towards the welfare of others, done without desiring any return for it whether of a temporal or spiritual nature. An 'act' here must be taken in its widest sense, and includes thought and word, as well as deed, 'others' embraces not only humanity but all life."[221] Gandhi said: "*yajna*, having come to us with our birth we are debtors all our lives, and thus for ever bound to serve the universe. And even as a bond slaves receives food, clothing and so on from the master whom he serves, so should we gratefully accept such gifts as may be assigned to us by the Lord of the Universe.

Decentralisation

For Gandhi *Khadi* and village industries stood for a decentralized economic system that can promote the economic and moral regeneration of the masses of India.[222] The depiction of Gandhi's ideas on decentralization would be incomplete if it is not mentioned that Gandhian economics is not based entirely on handicrafts and

219 Ibid., 132.

220 Ibid., 132.

221 Ibid., 144.

222 *Mahatma Gandhi's World-View*, 193.

cottage industries. Gandhi was not against large scale industries per se. On the other hand he admitted its due role and significance.

He visualized a balanced and organic relationship between the two sectors. In the Gandhi scheme,

> "Cottage and large scale industries were not competing alternatives but complementary and helpful to each other. Gandhi wanted small scale production and large industries to be developed in such a way that each sector will provide those supplies which cannot be produced by the other."[223]

Doctrine of Trusteeship

What is unique about Gandhian economic theory is that Gandhi did not accept the concept of ownership as such whether it be private or state. He considered both as equally exploitive and hence inconsistence with non-violence.[224] M.P. Mathai explains that Gandhi advised the owners of property to consider themselves as trustees of the property which really belonged to the whole society and manage it accordingly, taking only what they needed for their own upkeep but using the rest for the welfare of society.[225]

The Convergence

The striking points of convergence between the 4th century *theologian* and the 20th century *leader par-excellence* on the socio-economic sensitivity are assets for Indian context. One can with no trouble draw parallels in the Basilian social institution (e.g *Basiliad*) and Gandhian *Ashram* concept, the rejection of extravaganza and non-possession, extravaganza or non-sharing as theft etc. The Indian philosophical categories of thought in Gandhi vehemently nourish and compliment the 4th century Christian schema. The derived convergence serves to be a new paradigm for Indian context.

As Amartya Sen comments on the India's slow progress in removing social and economic inequality, he suggests that "this

223 *Mahatma Gandhi's World-View*, 194.

224 *Mahatma Gandhi's World-View*, 196.

225 *Mahatma Gandhi's World-View*, 197.

progress can be made more effective through committed public action and participatory activities" (*The Argumentative Indian*). What is required is an integrated approach to development and growth. Growth is not independent of the social transformation (of an economy).[226] And the converging paradigm of Basil and Gandhi provides a revitalized transformative approach.

Evaluation

The concerns of wealth and poverty, its legitimate purpose, catalyzed by recent economic recessions have all raised alarms for constructing a "just" and "enough" economic model. The Church in India has an issue at hand, to be dealt in detail drawing inspiration from the Patristic model as well as the Indian milieu. As an advocate and exponent of Social Justice St. Basil rightly describes the modern struggle with material wealth, concern for poor, liberation of the marginalized, and responsibility towards fellow human beings. Throughout his life Basil, remained committed to the cause of the poor and the socially exploited. He lived out the cause of poor with social commitments and exhortations thereby transforming the rich. Dwight Hopkins an African American theologian comments, "To be a Christian in any time period is to practice a preferential option for the poor."[227]

The converging Socio-economic paradigm in St. Basil and Gandhi possess the criticism of being philosophical, subjective and impractical. However, a space for critical re-examination of the socio-economic concerns linking poverty, wealth and ecology lies open for Theologizing in India.

226 http://www.livemint.com/Politics/hqZ776khE3VfUp9gbIdyML/Growth-alone-not-enough-to-fight-poverty-Amartya-Sen.html (12/08/2015).

227 Joerg Rieger. e.d., *Opting for the Margins: Postmodernity and Liberation in Christian Theology* (New York: OXFORD UNIVERSITY PRESS, 2003), 19.

Bibliography

Behr, John ed., *On the Holy Spirit*, Popular Patristics Series No. 42. New York: SVS Press, 2011.

Behr, John. *Formation of the Christian Theology. Vol. 2. The Nicene Faith Part 2*, New York: SVS Press, 2000.

Devadoss, T.S. *Sarvodaya*. Madras: University of Madras, 1974.

Holman, Susan R. e.d., *Wealth and Poverty in Early Church and Society*. U.S.A: Baker Academic, 2008.

Holman, Susan R. *The Hungry are Dying*. U.S.A: Oxford University Press, 2001.

Jurgens, William A. *The Faith of the Early Fathers*. Bangalore: TPI, 1992.

Kriplani, J.B. *Gandhian Thought*. Bombay: Orient Longmans, 1961.

Mathai, M.P., *Mahatma Gandhi's World-View*. New Delhi: Gandhi Peace Foundation, 2000.

Mathur, J.S. *Gandhian Thought and Contemporary Society*. e.d., Bombay: Bhartiya Vidya Bhavan, 1974.

Mshna, Rogate R. and Athena Peralta eds., *Linking Poverty, Wealth and Ecology*. Geneva: WCC Publications, 2013.

Pathil, Kuncheria and Veliath, Dominic: *An Introduction to Theology*. Bangalore: TPI, 2003.

Patil. V.T. e.d., *Studies on Gandhi*. New Delhi: Sterling Publishers, 1983.

Phan, Peter C. *Social Thought*. U.S.A: Michael Glazier, Inc, 1984.

Quasten, Johannes. *Patrology*. U.S.A: Christian Classics, 1996.

Ramachandran, G. & T.K. Mahadevan eds., *Gandhi*. New Delhi: Gandhi Peace Foundation, 1967.

Rieger. Joerg.e.d., *Opting for the Margins: Postmodernity and Liberation in Christian Theology*. OXFORD UNIVERSITY PRESS, 2003.

Rousseau, Philip. *Basil of Caesarea*. Berkley: University of California Press, 1994.

Schaff, Philip. *History of Christian Church. Vol. 3:* U.S.A: Hendrickson Publication, 2002.

Schaff, Philip, D.D, L.L.D, and Henry, Wace, eds., *Nicene and Post Nicene Fathers. Vol. 5*, U.S.A: Hendrickson Publication, 1999.

Schroeder, Paul C. *St. Basil on Social Justice.* Issue 38, 'Popular Patristic Series'. U.S.A: Vladimir's Seminary Press, 2009.

Sen, Amartya. *The Argumentative Indian.* New York: Farrar, Strauss, and Giroux, 2005.

Smith, Richard. *St. Basil the Great.* U.S.A: Kessinger Publishing, 2003.

Internet source

http://www.telegraph.co.uk/news/worldnews/asia/india/10003228/India-has-one-third-of-worlds-poorest-says-World-Bank.html (12/08/2015).

http://www.livemint.com/Politics/hqZ776khE3VfUp9gbIdyML/Growth-alone-not-enough-to-fight-poverty-Amartya-Sen.html (12/08/2015).

Appendix 3

Karl Rahner: I Believe in the Church

Introduction

Karl Rahner (1904-1984), born in feiburg im Breisgau, West Germany, was one of the greatest theologians of the 20st Century, a theologian par excellence. The Theological categories in his writings were wide spread and few prominent of them were Spirituality, Anthropology, Christology, Patristics, Trinity, Grace, Mission etc. We find in his works the dynamics of existentialism, spirituality, and pastoral concern. Rahner brings in the very intrinsic synthesis of scholastic, Dogmatic and Pastoral theology, a Theology in Praxis.

A *dialectical analogy* persists in Rahner as a method, dialectic between nature and grace, being & knowing, history & revelation, spirit & matter.[228] In Rahner, interestingly, Man is in himself an oscillation, a Schwebe;[229] he stands already at his goal, which is also his beginning, being, and yet he is not there. This notion of *Schwebe*,

228 Patrick Burke, *Reinterpreting Rahner: A Critical Study of His Major Themes* (New York: Fordham University Press, 2002), viii.

229 German word, literally meaning – *balance, to hover* or figuratively, *to hang in the balance.*

seemingly dominates Rahner's vision of reality and is the basis for the further development of his thought.[230]

I believe in the Church forms the last chapter of part one, *Fundamental Questions* of the Theological Investigations, Vol. VII. Here Rahner tries to answer a very poignant question for our times, how are the dogmatic definitions and assertions of the past relevant to us in the contemporary situation? While expounding the foundations of Ecclesiology Theology, Rahner deals with, Dogmatic, Sacramental, Scriptural and traditional aspects of Church. Ecclesiology was fundamental for Rahner and forms a major chunk of his theological writings with numerous books ascribed on the theme – Church. As Richard Lennan remarks, "The Church is the theme of over half of Karl rahner's writings.[231]

A Faith too Impatient

Karl Rahner urges for a patient attitude to dogmas and assertions made by the Church. Familiarity breeds contempt and Rahner in a similar vein points out "we hear these statements and know that what they are intended to convey. We have the impression that we know just as well as the speaker himself what he means, and yet we do not really take it in."[232]

Further, Rahner emphatically elucidates that we are not unbelievers, but it seems we are, as it were susceptible to an overdose of the light of faith. He adds, Faith is not difficult to us of today on the grounds that we can explain things sufficiently without it, but because faith itself seems to us to be trying to explain more than we can bear. [233]

Epistemology: 'New' Knowledge

Rahner explicitly points out the reluctance of acquiring any 'new' knowledge, and what is new is always unfamiliar and frightening.

230 Burke, *Reinterpreting Rahner*, 43.

231 Richard Lennan, *The Ecclesiology of Karl Rahner* (Oxford: Clarendon Press, 1997), 10.

232 *Theological Investigations* Vol. II, Karl Rahner, Translated by David Bourke (London: 1971), 100.

233 *Ibid.*, 101.

The only thing we hope to gain from the acquisition of any 'new' knowledge is to confirm ourselves I our existing position: 'That is precisely as I had already thought'[234] For Rahner real truths, however, when they make their initial impact upon us, make us shy away. They carry further implication beyond themselves; they threaten us, change us, or even challenge us beyond accustomed areas of thought.[235] Rahner explains that when we are tempted to reduce the truth of God in its greatness to the petty dimensions of human 'truth', then first encounter with word of God would always be blinding and dazzling by its brilliance, bewildering and upsetting because of the fact that that it is so immeasurably above us.[236]

There are various human reasons pointed out by Rahner to objecting or resisting the truth of God, however for him they are mere derivations from the guise of lowliness and abasement in which word of God has become incarnate and human, and in which it still continues to do so ever anew.[237] Rahner is of the opinion that truth of God doesn't always come just as a kind of poetic consolation or a devotional story for children as for few as miracles of grace, but the grace of faith can work as well in an obstinate spirit and a rebellious heart, as God usually performs his greatest miracles.

The recognition that the truth of God, even when it really is the truth of God, does not necessarily 'suit' us. And it does not suit us because we do not suit it until we have altered ourselves in order to do so. The attitude of patient attentiveness, endurance involved in learning something new, readiness for change, humility of a sensitive spirit.[238] Thus, after an introspective and subjective sphere, Rahner leads the discussions into an objective sphere, outside ourselves, the Church.

---

234 Rahner, *Theological Investigations Vol. VII.*, 103.

235 Ibid., 103.

236 Ibid., 103.

237 Ibid., 105.

238 Ibid., 105.

The Church: The Object & Dimension of Our Faith

The Church is the object of our faith, and in a mysterious way, at the same time also the dimension in which it exists. Rahner explains the two complementary dimensions of inner and outer sphere of faith. He writes, "The two aspects are mutually complementary, and it makes no difference to our present argument at which of the two points the actual act of faith on the part of the individual is initiated in the concrete: whether he believes in the Church first and then in the rest of the matters proposed for his belief because these come from the Church, or whether he first attains to belief in Christ and his word, and goes on from there to belief in the Church as founded by Christ."[239]

Church as Mystery

In Rahner's theological categories, God is a mystery and this mystery is projected through the parlance of incomprehensibility of God. However, when this mystery is also the nature of the Holy Church, thus it means objectification is impossible. No sociological analysis will ever do full justice to the Church. If Church is Mystery, it follows that a correct understanding of the Church is only possible in faith. Faith that furthers and evolves itself through the spirit and the word by into the Church. Interestingly, as John J. O'Donnell puts it, 'in the creed, the believer's profession of faith in the Church comes under the third article, belief in the Holy Spirit. Only the Holy Spirit or grace makes faith in the Church possible.'[240] As Christians we believe in that word that comes to us from the incarnate Word of the Father, Jesus Christ. And He is at once the head, the foundation stone, and the architect of that entity, visible yet so mysterious, which we call the Church.[241] Church as Mystery- and the openness to Mystery remains as a horizon of ever greater possibility for reception of grace, through self communication of God's own self.

239 Rahner, *Theological Investigations Vol. VII,* 106.

240 John J. O' Donnell, e.d., *Karl Rahner: Life in the Spirit* (Rome: Gregorian University Press, 2004), 67.

241 Rahner, *Theological Investigations Vol. VII*, 107.

Rahner explains that through the incarnational & salvific history, This divine reality, Spirit, grace, truth, compassion and love of God, which is the most real factor in the world, however much it may be hidden, is brought about by God through Christ, through his Body, through his word, and his commandment, through the authority derived from him, through his sacraments in their palpable and physical reality, their concrete apprehensible presence in the here and now.[242] Rahner conveys that the utmost manifestations of grace are available through church to us by the means of Sacraments. It reminds of a Sacramental theology definition, 'sacraments are the visible manifestations of the invisible grace. "So we are believers, hearers of the word of God as found in the mouth of the Church. What the Church says is our light and our strength, the love of the living God in spite of all the darkness."[243] And from the mouth of the Church handed down to us through ministers in the word of God, both written and proclaimed, and in the visible sacraments of the Church.[244]

The faith & its concerns have a pivotal aspect in Church, Church as the fellowship of faithful isn't merely the sum total of those who believe, rather it inculcates a priority over the belief of the individual. It supplies the support and the basis of that belief.[245] Rahner succinctly explains the corporate nature of faith; Faith is only complete and truly possible in the community of the faithful, in the Church. Faith doesn't only mean accepting what 'I' as an individual believe that I have heard. It also means accepting what the Church has heard, giving my assent to the 'confession' of the Church.[246] Rahner envisages a Church in the Christian understanding of faith and of human existence. The Church for Rahner is not the ideological creation of a religious enthusiasm, nor of the religious experience of an individual. It is received through history, in the concreteness of his life, developed from a community of persons,

242 Ibid., 107.

243 Ibid., 102.

244 Ibid., 102.

245 Ibid., 109.

246 Rahner, *Theological Investigations Vol. VII*, 110.

from intercommunication, from an objective spirit, from a history and within this community.[247]

Conclusion

Essentially, for Rahner his spiritual rootedness leads to Theology, and in this scheme, anthropology is often his starting point. The *anthropological turn* is indeed the way to better understanding of God, Christ and bridging the gap between Transcendence and Historical, Transcendence with the here & now. In the chapter too, Rahner seems to be echoing the anthropological basis even while expounding the ecclesiological stance of the Church. Man – Faith-individual and corporate nature of ecclesia, all seem to highlight the anthropological turn ever prevalent in Rahner.

Rahner in this chapter seems to be in an apologetic fervor, and as an ardent catholic theologian upholding traditional creeds and at the same time reinterpreting with contemporary values. Rahner doesn't just provide a theoretical instruction alone through his writings, but rather assists & leads one to experience grace. A reader often undergoes pathos and a purging all the way through the pages of Rahner's works. Indeed, one of the greatest synthetic thinkers of the twentieth century, very dynamic and dialectic while theologizing the greatest concerns of our world.

Few important facets of Rahner's ecclesiology can be recognized in these words, "This Church always continues to be a living Church not only because there really takes place within it faith, hope and love, not only because the Lord's supper is celebrated and his death is proclaimed, but also because the real thing which constitutes the church does manifest again and again in a way which is sufficient for anyone who looks at the church with an open heart and with the eyes of faith."[248] Faithful to the Church's tradition, Rahner was nonetheless convinced of the Church's need to reform its structures and clarify its doctrines in order to respond. To locate Rahnerian ecclesiology which envisions a church committed to preservation of its heritage and an openness to change.

247 Karl Rahner, *Foundations of Christian Faith*, trans. William V. Dych (London: Darton Longman & Todd, 1978), 389.

248 Rahner, *Foundations of Christian Faith*, 390.

Bibliography

Burke, Patrick. *Reinterpreting Rahner*. New York: Fordham University Press, 2002.

Lennan, Richard. *The Ecclesiology of Karl Rahner*. Oxford: Clarendon Press, 1997.

Marmion, Declan & Mary E. Hines, eds. *The Cambridge Companion to Karl Rahner*. Cambridge: Cambridge University Press, 2005.

O' Donnell, John J. e.d. *Karl Rahner: Life in the Spirit*. Rome: Gregorian University Press, 2004.

Rahner, Karl. *Encounters with Silence*. Translated by James M. Demske. New York: Newman Press, 1960.

Rahner, Karl. *Foundations of Christian Faith*. Translated by William V. Dych. London: Darton Longman & Todd, 1978.

Rahner, Karl. *Theological Investigations Vol. II*. Translated by David Bourke. London: 1971.

Appendix 4

Paul Ricoeur: Role of Reason in Interaction with Faith

Paul Ricoeur (1913-2005), is certainly one of the most challenging and enduring thinker of 20th century. Ricoeur's major hermeneutical works from the 1950s to the present day have been devoted to the interpretation of the 'mediations' of meaning through symbol, myth, dream, image, text, narrative and ideology.[249] By his own account, the central motif of his philosophy is: "Detour/return is the rhythm of my philosophical respiration." The pattern is so pervasive that it shaped the trajectory of his entire career: a philosophy of the will that detours through analyses of sign, symbol, metaphor, and narrative, returning to a richer account of personal identity in his hermeneutics of the self.[250]

Oneself as Another (1990)

Oneself as Another, catalysis a hermeneutics of the self, that charts its epistemological path and ontological status. It suggests from the outset that the selfhood of oneself implies otherness to such an

249 Richard Kearney, *On Paul Ricoeur: The Owl of Minerva* (England: Ashgate Publishing Limited, 2004), 13.

250 Boyd Blundell, *Paul Ricoeur between Theology and Philosophy: Detour and Return* (U.S.A: Indiana University Press, 2010), 2.

intimate degree that one cannot be thought of without the other, that instead one passes into the other, as we might say in Hegelian terms.[251] Ricoeur believes, in its very stubbornness to want to doubt, it confirms its will to certainty and to truth, thus giving doubt as such a kind of direction: in this sense, Cartesian doubt is not Kierkegaardian despair. Quite the opposite, the will to discover is what motivates it; what I want to discover is the truth of things themselves.[252] For Ricoeur the Cartesian cogito or doubt is more affirming to the fact of "certain and indubitable." The hyposthesis of the evil genius as great deceiver is also pivotal, as the deceit consists precisely in making seeming pass for "true being." Through doubt, 'I will believe that none of those things…ever existed'; what I want to discover is "is one thing that is certain and indubitable."[253]

The hermeneutic self for Ricoeur is not a self-sufficient *cogito* but an incarnate being which discovers that it is placed in language before it possesses itself in consciousness. Human being, for Ricoeur, is always, a *being-intrepreted.* It cannot start from itself or simply invent meanings out of itself *ex nihilo*. Therefore, instead of proceeding according to the model of Cartesian *concept*-a pure and distinct idea transparent to itself- hermeneutics is committed to the primacy of the *symbol,* where meaning emerges as oblique, mediated, enigmatic, layered, and multiform. 'In contrast to philosophies concerned with starting points', Ricoeur explains, 'a meditation on symbols starts from the fullness of language and of meaning already there; it begins from within language which has already taken place and in which everything in a certain sense has already been said; it wants to be thought, not presuppositionless, but in and with all its presuppositions. Its first problem is not how to get started, but from the midst of speech to recollect itself.'[254]

---

251 Paul Ricoeur, *Oneself as Another*, Translated by Kathleen Blamey (Chicago: The University of Chicago Press, 1992), 3.

252 Ricoeur, *Oneself and Another,* 6.

253 Ibid., 6.

254 Kearney, *On Paul Ricoeur*, 14.

The Summoned Self

The lecture "The summoned Subject in the School of the Narratives of the Prophetic Vocation" as Ricouer explains, has to be understood and read as a continuation specifically to "The Self in the Mirror of Scripture" and broadly with "Oneself as Another."[255] For Ricoeur, self is constituted and defined by its position as respondent. It is in stark opposition to the philosophical hubris of a self that absolutely names itself. Self that responds is a self in relation, without being an absolute self- that is, outside any relatedness and in this sense the foundation of every relation. Ricoeur adds, the phrase "summoned self" indicates the place of a certain congruence with the self described in a hermeneutics of the "I am". This "I am", in its broad outlines is already a self in relation and, in this way, a self in the position of respondent.[256]

Paul Ricoeur delineates Rene Descartes' *Meditations* to bring out the subtle notion of the infinite. On the first truth immediately known by reflecting on doubt and order of reasons Ricoeur reflects that the 'Third Meditation' reverses the order (order of discovery, *ordo cognoscendi*) and slips to the second ontological rank by placing the certainty of the cogito in a subordinate position in relation to divine veracity, which is first in accordance with the "truth of the thing."[257] He believes cogito would be genuinely absolute in all respects if it could be shown that there is but one order, that in which it is indeed first, and that the other order, in which it is set back to second place, derives from the first.[258]

Ricoeur explicates the idea of myself and that of God, and quotes Descartes, "Thus the [notion] of the infinite somehow exists in me prior to the [notion] of the finite, that is, the [notion] of God exists prior to the [notion] of myself." (*Third Meditation*). One must Ricoeur opines, therefore go so far as to say that, if God is the *ratio essendi* of myself, he thereby becomes the *ratio cognoscendi* of

---

255 David F. Ford, Mike Higton & Simeon Zahl, eds., *The Modern Theologians Reader* (U.K: Blackwell Publishing Ltd., 2012), 174.

256 *The Modern Theologians Reader*, 174.

257 Ricoeur, *Oneself and Another*, 8.

258 Ibid.

myself, since I am an imperfect being, a being who is lacking; the imperfection attaching to doubt is known only by the light of the idea of perfection.[259]

Narratives of Prophetic Call

Ricoeur uses various narratives of the prophetic call or vocation in the Old Testament as first figure of a responding self. For these 'quasi-autobiographical' narratives 'A *Sitz-im-Wort* (setting in the word) succeeds a *Sitz-im-Leben*' (sociological setting).[260] The various phases are identified in these calling and commissioning narratives. Moreover, for Ricouer the dialogic structure, although asymmetric- of the commissioning is sealed by the word of "reassurance": "I will be with you in truth", "Go I am with you" "I will open your mouth", commanding and establishing the prophet to listen in order to speak.[261] Ricouer further explains that the communal aspect of the commission cannot be blocked out by the solitude of the call; one is called, a whole people is intended.[262]

Under the category 'summoned self', the Old Testament prophetic narratives' parallel found and is enriched in Pauline theology of the 'Christomorphic self'. In Ricoeur, the Paradigm of believer being transformed into the Christ image, in contrast with the *Imagio Dei* in Adam (Genesis 1:26) and moving towards grandeur of the 'glory'- the glory of Yahweh (Exodus 24:15-16) is inevitable. Interestingly, a chain of glory as Ricoeur presents is- God's glory, that of Christ, that of the Christian. Furthermore, Ricoeur exploring the testimony of conscience he argues that the testimony of conscience is an internal dialogue, an address in part to itself, and that the testimony of conscience precedes the accusation of conscience. Ricoeur draws from Pauline dialectic between knowledge shared within oneself (*suneidesis* / conscience) and the Christian Kerygma (*Justification of faith*). A theology of conscience for Ricoeur requires a

259 Ricoeur, *Oneself and Another*, 9.

260 *The Modern Theologians Reader*, 175.

261 Ibid., 176.

262 *The Modern Theologians Reader*, 176.

simultaneous reinterpretation of the phenomenon of conscience and of the Christian kerygma.[263]

Conclusion

Paul Ricoeur was simultaneously faithful to what he called "biblical faith" and to an acknowledged "agnosticism" in philosophy. Although, he was willing to engage the two disciplines or discourses with each other to different degrees at various points of his career, most of the time he kept them rigorously separate. As Ricoeur remarks in the introduction of *Oneself as Another*, the primary reason for exclusion of the twin lectures (*The self in the mirror of Scripture* and *The mandated self*, from *Oneself as Another*) is his concern to pursue, to the very last line, an autonomous, philosophical discourse.[264] Peculiarly, the influence of Christian faith is irrevocable in Ricoeur', he writes explaining the genesis of the title, *Oneself as Another* 'I therefore retained as the title of the book that was to emerge from Gifford Lectures the expression, Oneself as Another; the lineaments of which I found in the magnificent lines that conclude Bernanos's *Diary of a Country Priest*: It is easier than one thinks to hate oneself. Grace is to forget oneself. But, if all pride were dead in us, the grace of all graces would be to love oneself humbly, as any of the suffering members of Jesus Christ.'[265] How can modern readers truly engage the biblical worldview when it is so foreign to their own way of thinking and perceiving? For Paul Ricoeur, a meaningful encounter between reader and traditional text is still possible, but it can only come indirectly: the reader must first go through a conscious process of interpretation. Biblical narratives aren't much historical, literal account; rather, it is the language of mythic and symbolic foundational stories to express the encounters with the divine. As Ricoeur puts it, "the symbol gives rise to thought." Ricoeur formulates a hermeneutical circle: "we

263 Ibid., 178.

264 Ricoeur, *Oneself and Another*, 24.

265 Lewis Edwin Hahn, ed., *Philosophy of Paul Ricoeur* (U.S.A: Open Court Publishing, 1995), 50.

must understand in order to believe, but we must believe in order to understand."[266]

Ricoeur's method of 'dialetical' and critical hermeneutics is very innovative as the immediate context of a biblical hermeneutics was not essentially an externally critical hermeneutics – it certainly took for granted a certain history of salvation. As Christianity is at its core both historical and textual, the pattern of detour and return is pervasive throughout theology. From the Gospels and Epistles to the creeds and councils, theological reflection has functioned as a detour, finding its source in what God has done in the world through Jesus Christ and seeking to return to the world by orienting the lives of Christians.[267]

Ricoeur often engages with the text or source within a hermeneutic loop where meaning emerges through the continual revolving from text, author, and reader, past and present interpretations, larger context and contemporary scope. Reason interacts with faith in Ricoeur in a peculiar manner, dialectically engaging, challenging and enriching mutually. He carefully delineates the different kinds of texts and genres contained in the biblical patterns deeply woven into the fabric of lived experience. Also, in Ricoeur the binary oppositions never oversimplifies and the binarity is never a set of equivalences; Philosophy versus Theology, ethics versus politics, discourse versus action. There is always a complex matrix of differences which, when it fits, does so in terms of a mosaic-like result. The differences permeate into patterns as its splendor and enriches reciprocally.[268]

---

266 Martin Albl, *Reason, Faith and Tradition* (U.S.A: Saint Mary's Press, 2009), 62-64.

267 Blundell, *Paul Ricoeur between Theology and Philosophy*, 3.

268 Hahn, ed., *Philosophy of Paul Ricoeur*, 67.

Bibliography

Blundell, Boyd. *Paul Ricoeur between Theology and Philosophy: Detour and Return*. U.S.A: Indiana University Press, 2010.

Edwin Hahn, Lewis., ed. *Philosophy of Paul Ricoeur.* U.S.A: Open Court Publishing, 1995.

Ford, David F., Mike Higton & Simeon Zahl., eds. *The Modern Theologians Reader*. U.K: Blackwell Publishing Ltd., 2012.

Gschwandtner, Christina M. "Paul Ricœur and the Relationship Between Philosophy and Religion in Contemporary French Phenomenology."

Kearney, Richard. *On Paul Ricoeur*. England: Ashgate Publishing Limited, 2004.

Ricoeur, Paul. *Oneself as Another*. Translated by Kathleen Blamey. Chicago: The University of Chicago Press, 1992.

Ricœur Studies, Vol 3, No 2 (2012), pp. 7-25, https://ricoeur.pitt.edu/ojs/index.php/ricoeur/article/viewFile/147/64

Bibliography

Ashwin, Piotr-Siejkowski. *Clement of Alexandria*. New York: T & T Clark, 2008.

__________. *Clement of Alexandria on Trial.* Boston: Brill, 2010.

Bauer, W. *Orthodoxy and Heresy in Earliest Christianity*. London: SCM Press Ltd., 1972.

Baumer, Bettina, ed., *Kalatattvakosa. Vol. II*. New Delhi: Indira Gandhi National Centre for the Arts, 2003.

Behr, John. *Asceticism and Anthropology in Irenaeus and Clement.* London: Oxford University Press, 2000.

Benedict XVI, Pope. *Church Fathers.* Bangalore: Asian Trading Corporation, 2010.

Bettenson, Henry, ed., *Early Christian Fathers.* New York: Oxford University Press, 1956.

Bhattacharya, Ashim Kumar. *Hindu Dharma*. New York: IUniverse, Inc., 2006.

Brubaker, Pamela and Rogate Mshana, eds. *Justice Not Greed.* Geneva: WCC Publication, 2010.

Bultmann, Rudolf. *Primitive Christianity*. Cleveland: The World Publishing Company, 1963.

Burnouf, Eugene. *Introduction to the History of Indian Buddhism.* Chicago: The University of Chicago Press, 2010.

Butterworth, G. W. *Clement of Alexandria*. London: Harvard University Press, 1919.

Carter, Robert E. ed., *God the Self and Nothingness*. New York: Paragon House, 1990.

Chadwick, H. ed., *Alexandrian Christianity*. Philadelphia: The Westminster Press, 1950.

__________. *Early Christian Thought and Classical Tradition*. London: Clarendon Press, 1966.

Copleston, Fredrick. *A History of Philosophy, Vol. I*. New York: Image Books, 1962.

Cross, F. L. *The Early Christian Fathers*. London: Gerald Duckworth & Co. Ltd., 1960.

Culloch, Diarmaid Mac. *A History of Christianity*. London: Penguin Books, 2010.

Desrochers, John. *India's Growing Slums*. Bangalore: Centre for Social Action, 2000.

Dowing, F. Gerald. *Cynics, Paul and the Pauline Churches*. London: Routledge, 1998.

Ferguson, John. *Clement of Alexandria*. U.S.A: Twayne Publishers, 1974.

Floyd, W.E.G. *Clement of Alexandria's Treatment of the Problem of Evil*. London: Oxford University Press, 1971.

Foster, Richard J. *Freedom of Simplicity*. New York: Harper & Row Publishers, 1981.

Frend, W.H.C. *The Rise of Christianity*. Philadelphia: Fortress Press, 1984.

Fuller, B.A.G. *A History of Philosophy*. New York: Henry Holt and Company, 1938.

George, K.M. *Philosophy East and West*. Kottayam: Mar Gregorios Foundation, 2013.

Grenz, Stanley J. *The Social God and the Relational Self*. London: Westminster John Knox Press, 2001.

Grimm, Veronika E. *From Feasting to Fasting, The Evolution of a Sin.* London: Routledge, 1996.

Hagg, Henny Fiska. *Clement of Alexandria and the Beginnings of Christian Apophaticism.* New York: Oxford University Press, 2006.

Hengel, Martin. *Property and Riches in the Early Church.* London: SCM Press, 1974.

Holman, Susan R. ed., *Wealth and Poverty in Early Church and Society.* U.S.A: Baker Academic, 2008.

__________. *The Hungry are Dying.* U.S.A: Oxford University Press, 2001.

Itter, Andrew C. *Esoteric Teaching in the Stromateis of Clement of Alexandria.* Boston: Brill Publications, 2009.

Iyer, R. ed. *The Essential Writings of Mahatma Gandhi.* New Delhi; Oxford University Press, 1994.

Jaeger, Werner. *Early Christianity and Greek Paideia.* London: Oxford University Press, 1977.

Jha, Urga Mohan, ed., *Rural Development in India.* New Delhi: Anmol Publications, 1995.

Juergensmeyer, Mark and Wade Clark Roof, eds. *Encyclopedia of Global Religions.* London: Sage Publications, 2012.

Jurgens, William A. *The Faith of the Early Fathers, Vol. I.* Bangalore: TPI, 1992.

Kelly, J. N. D. *Early Christian Doctrine.* London: A & C. Black, 1958.

Klauck, Hans Josef. *The Religious Context of Early Christianity.* London: T & T Clark Ltd., 2000.

Konrad Raiser. *Theological Considerations Regarding a Wealth/ Greed Line.* A paper prepared for a consultation in Geneva, 7 December 2009.

Kraft, H. *Early Christian Thinkers.* London: Lutterworth Press, 1964.

Kumarappa, J. C. *Gandhian Economic Thought* .Varanasi: Sarva Seva Sangh Prakashan, 1951.

Lilla, S.R.C., *Clement of Alexandria: A Study in Christian Platonism and Gnosticsm*. Oxford: OUP, 1971.

Long, A. A. *Cambridge Companion to: Early Greek Philosophy*. U.K: Cambridge University Press, 1999.

Mashana, Rogate R. and Athena Peralta, eds. *Linking Poverty, Wealth and Ecology*. Geneva: WCC, 2013.

Mehat, A. *Etude sur les 'Stromates' de Clement d'Alexandrie*. Paris: Du Seuil, 1966.

Niebuhr, H. Richard. *The Responsible Self*. San Francisco: Harper and Row Publishers, 1978.

Osborn, Eric. *Clement of Alexandria*. U.K: Cambridge University Press, 2005.

__________. *The Philosophy of Clement of Alexandria*. U.K: Cambridge University Press, 1957.

Pears, Angie. *Doing Contextual Theology*. New York: Routledge, 2010.

Peralta, Athena and Rogate R. Mshana, eds. *The Greed Line*. Geneva: WCC Publications, 2014.

Phan, Peter C. *Social Thought*. U.S.A: Michael Glazier, Inc, 1984.

Quasten, Johannes. *Patrology*. U.S.A: Christian Classics, 1996.

Rainy, Robert. *The Ancient Catholic Church*. New York: Charles Scribners's Sons, 1902.

Roskam, Geert. *On the Path to Virtue*. Belgium: Leuven University Press, 2005.

Russell, Norman. *The Doctrine of Deification in the Greek Patristic Tradition*. New York: Oxford University Press, 2004.

Schaff, Philip, D. D, L.L.D, and Henry Wace, eds., *Nicene and Post Nicene Fathers. Vol. 1*, U.S.A: Hendrickson Publication, 1999.

Sharp, Andrew M. *Orthodox Christians and Islam in Postmodern Age*. The Netherlands: Brill Publications, 2012.

Shepherd, Andrew. *The Gift of the Other*. Cambridge: James Clarke & Co., 2014.

Strachey, Majorie. *The Fathers without Theology*. New York: George Braziller Inc., 1958.

Whitacre, A. Rodney. *A Patristic Greek Reader*. Massachusetts: Hendrickson Publishers, 2007.

Williams, M. Monier. *Buddhism*. New Delhi: Munshiram Manoharlal Publishers, 1995.

Wolfson, Harry Austryn. *The Philosophy of the Church Fathers. Vol. I.* Cambridge: Harvard University Press, 1956.

Wood, James. Transl., *The Yoga System of Patanjali.* U.K: Harvard University Press, 2003.

Wyschogrod, Edith, David Crownfield and Carl A. Raschke, eds. *Lacan and Theological Discourse.* New York: State University of New York Press, 1989.

Young, Frances, Lewis Aryes and Andrew Louth eds., *The Cambridge History of Early Christian Literature.* U.K: Cambridge University Press, 2004.

Zizioulas, John D. *Communion and Otherness.* London: T & T Clark, 2006.

__________. *The One and the Many.* California: Sebastian Press, 2010.

The Ecumenical Review. Oxford: Blackwell Publishing. October, 2011.

"*The writings of Clement of Alexandria*", Vol. I. Translated by William Wilson. In *Ante-Nicene Christian Library*, edited by Alexander Roberts and James Donaldson. Edinburgh: T & T Clark, 1869.

The writings of Clement of Alexandria, Vol. II. Translated by William Wilson. In *Ante-Nicene Christian Library*, edited by Alexander Roberts and James Donaldson. Edinburgh: T & T Clark, 1869.

Fathers of the Church, Vol. 23. Translated by Simon P. Wood. U.S.A: The Catholic University of America Press, 1954.

Sustainable Alernatives for Poverty Reduction and Eco-Justice. Lucas Andrianos, Jan-Willem Sneep, Guillermo Kerber and Robin Attfield. U.K: Cambridge Scholars Publishing, 2014.

Journal

Maier, Harry O. "Clement of Alexandria and the Care of the Self." *Journal of the American Academy of Religion LXII/3*, Vol. 62, No. 3 (Autumn, 1994): 22-31.

Documents and Reports

The Millenium Development Goals Report (United Nations Secretariat). Department of Economic and Social Affairs. United Nations. 2015.

Konrad Raiser. *Theological Considerations Regarding a Wealth/ Greed Line*. A paper prepared for a consultation in Geneva, 7 December 2009.

Rossarin. *Happiness and Public Policy*. A paper presented at international conference organized by the Public Policy Development Office (PPDO), the Government House, Bangkok and the United Nations Economic and Social Commission for Asia and the Pacific (UNESCAP), in Bangkok, Thailand, 18-19 July 2007.

Internet Resources

http://www.earlychristianwritings.com/text/clement-richman.html (10/2/2015).

http://www.telegraph.co.uk/news/worldnews/asia/india/10003228/India-has-one-third-of-worlds-poorest-says-World-Bank.html (12/08/2015).

http://timesofindia.indiatimes.com/india/30-crore-people-still-live-in-extreme-poverty-in-India-UN-report/articleshow/46122767.cms (12/08/2015).

http://www.livemint.com/Politics/hqZ776khE3VfUp9gbIdyML/Growth-alone-not-enough-to-fight-poverty-Amartya-Sen.html (12/08/2015).

http://books.google.co.in/books?id= -r87AAAAcAAJ&pg= PA539&dq=clement+of+alexandria+%2B+self+sufficiency&hl=en&sa=X&ei=J8YoVLSnGsaRuATu14LYCA&ved=0CDEQ6AEwBA#v=o

nepage&q=clement%20of%20alexandria%20%2B%20self%20sufficiency&f=false (10/10/2015).

http://www.academia.edu/3214435/The_Greek_Christian_fathers (11/10/2015).

http://books.google.co.in/books?id=igAujkCmoMC&pg=PA94&lpg=PA94&dq=clement+of+alexandria+%2B+wealth&source=bl&ots=8B3gayWspb&sig=vtHBeUz41xkf1lORSFFnh6AY98&hl=en&sa=X&ei=e50lVI71OpPhuQTNz4GABw&ved=0CFUQ6AEwCA#v=onepage&q=clement%20of%20alexandria%20%2B%20wealth&f=false (12/10/2015).

https://ejournals.bc.edu/ojs/index.php/ctsa/article/download/3014/2633 (16/10/2015).

http://www.academia.edu/3214435/The_Greek_Christian_fathers (20/10/2015).

http://books.google.co.in/books?id=0cM9wDXYvgC&pg=PA191&lpg=PA191&dq=st.clement+of+alexandria+%2B+autarky (4/11/2015).

https://ia600302.us.archive.org/15/items/clementofalexand00clem/clementofalexand00clem.pdf (10/11/2015).

https://books.google.co.in/books?id=45pfB4VaoAIC&pg=PR3&source=gbs_selected_pages&cad=3#v=onepage&q&f=false (10/11/2015).

https://www.academia.edu/835571/Monograph_Clement_of_Alexandria_on_trial_the_evidence_of_heresy_from_Photius_Bibliotheca (10/11/2015).

https://books.google.co.in/books?id=aepYpUVf9OkC&pg=PA120&lpg=PA120&dq=Didascalus+clement&source=bl&ots=SdBeWuUXsW&sig=ez05h8n1S10NNKJrQm1bPYtwyEw&hl=en&sa=X&ved=0ahUKEwj1zfal3_nKAhVnIKYKHRA8CAsQ6AEIOTAG#v=onepage&q=Didascalus%20clement&f=false (11/11/2015).

http://ext.sagepub.com/content/124/8/405.extract# (15/11/2015).

http://www.britannica.com/biography/Saint-Clement-of-Alexandria (28/11/2015).

http://www.un.org/millenniumgoals/2015_MDG_Report/pdf/MDG%202015%20rev%20(July%201).pdf (1/12/2015).

http://www.ccel.org/ccel/wace/biodict.html?term=Clement%20of%20Alexandria (1/12/2015).

http://www.orthodoxebooks.org/node/282 (17/12/2015).

http://www.hetsa.org.au/pdf/35-A-3.pdf (28/12/2015).

http://www.pub22.net/avilla/Republic.html (28/12/2015).

http://www.theguardian.com/theguardian/2007/may/01/greatspeeches (09/01/2016).

https://archive.org/details/nighantuniruktao00yaskuoft (10/1/16).

http://www.cs.mcgill.ca/~rwest/link-suggestion/wpcd_2008-09_augmented/wp/g/Greco-Buddhism.htm (10/1/2016).

http://www.happysociety.org/ppdoconference/session_papers/session17/session17_rossarin.pdf (11/01/2016).

http://books.google.co.in/books?id=XEuddWHIqaYC&pg=PA383&lpg=PA383&dq=autarchy+%2B+early+christian&source=bl&ots=ANeiMVjKBx&sig=GzpgmEYfTW6184XrQToCKQJyhuM&hl=en&sa=X&ei=Ul4sVI_eOZSOuATExIDYAQ&ved=0CDoQ6AEwBw#v=onepage&q=autarchy%20%2B%20early%20christian&f=false (22/01/2016).